WILLIAM COWPER: THE CONTINUING REVALUATION

WILLIAM COWPER

THE CONTINUING REVALUATION

AN ESSAY AND A BIBLIOGRAPHY
OF COWPERIAN STUDIES
from 1895 to 1960

By

LODWICK HARTLEY

Chapel Hill
THE UNIVERSITY OF NORTH CAROLINA PRESS
1960

PRINTED IN THE UNITED STATES OF AMERICA
BY THE SEEMAN PRINTERY, DURHAM, N. C.

To

F. H. B.

in sincere appreciation

PREFACE

THE INCEPTION OF THE present work lies in a movement to bring out pamphlet check lists of studies in eighteenth-century English literature that was begun over a decade ago. Early pamphlets in the somewhat informal series included, among others, lists prepared by Professors James E. Tobin, Louis A. Landa, and Francesco Cordasco on such figures as Alexander Pope, Jonathan Swift, and Laurence Sterne. The emphasis was particularly on books, magazine articles, and other studies that had appeared during the preceding half-century. My own list published in 1950 was designed to perform a similar service for studies of William Cowper beginning with 1895, the date that Professor Tobin had already selected as a convenient one, not only for his bibliography of Pope published in 1945, but also for his earlier *Eighteenth Century English Literature and Its Cultural Background; A Bibliography*, which appeared in 1939 and for two decades has been a standard tool of scholarship.

Since the CBEL bibliography of Cowper was scanty as a whole (especially in listing studies appearing after 1935), since its inadequacy was only partially remedied by the recent *Supplement*, and since no other extensive list was available, a steady and a gratifyingly widespread demand for my list developed. The original printing has for some time been exhausted. Furthermore, another decade has elapsed in which activity in Cowperian scholarship has been considerable.

The continued interest in eighteenth-century bibliographical aids, particularly as evidenced by the reception of Professor James L. Clifford's indispensable *Johnsonian Studies* of 1951 and the happy persistence of Cowperian studies, has, therefore, led me to make a thoroughgoing revision and expansion of my original list with the hope of providing a more reliable and a far more elaborate basis for fruitful scholarship in the future.

In the main, I have followed the format of the other bibliographies in the field—most specifically in the matter of consecutively numbered references with the inclusion of cross references when they have seemed necessary to the solution of some of the difficult problems of classification or when they have seemed pertinent to a body of significant material involved. My chief departure from my own and from other lists has been in the extensive annotation. By such annotation I have hoped to indicate succinctly and significantly the contents of the items included or the tenor of the opinions expressed in them. To do the latter, I have often resorted to direct quotation. In addition to providing a practical and clear guide to the studies included, the annotation is intended to contribute to the readability of the list—a quality not often attributed to, or demanded of, bibliographies, but one which certainly cannot be regarded as deterrent to the stimulation of interest in the subject.

The scope and purpose of the prefatory chapters will be apparent from the table of contents. They are designed to review briefly the whole background of critical opinion, to summarize (with more cohesion than even an annotated bibliography could hope for) the significant literature concerning the poet, and, as a conclusion, to consider once more the most important elements contributing to his permanence.

Since completely orthodox notation of these chapters would have necessitated a separate list of those books earlier than 1895 that are mentioned in the discussion and since such a plan of double bibliography appeared to offer more confusion than enlightenment, I have referred by superscript numbers in the text only to the items covered within the scope of the bibliography itself. Other sources are indicated as plainly as possible without resort to further apparatus.

With the desire to be as complete as possible (an ideal never, of course, fully achieved), I have included many minor items—critical and otherwise. Thus one may find a note on a collection of twigs ostensibly preserved from Cowper's garden, a comment on the poet's prophecy of human flight, or an appreciation of the poetry that is a poor medley of second- or third-hand opinions. These items, however, have been labeled carefully enough so that future researchers may dispose of them without further ado. The really important entries should be clearly apparent both from the comment in the introductory chapters and from individual annotation.

In my earlier list, I gratefully acknowledged the aid of Professors Hoxie N. Fairchild, Neilson C. Hannay, and Maurice Quinlan. To these I am still indebted. I am also glad to add Professor Charles Ryskamp of Princeton University, who provided a valuable list of additions and corrections to the original list; Dr. H. K. Gregory of the Case Institute of Technology, who contributed an excellent abstract of Boutin's medico-psychological monograph; and Mrs. Norma Hodgson Russell, Librarian of Somerville College, Oxford, who has given assistance in bibliographical details.

The staff of the D. H. Hill Library at North Carolina State College and the staff of the University of North Carolina Press have provided efficient and indispensable technical assistance. I owe a particular debt to two of my colleagues, Professors Herbert G. Eldridge and A. Sidney Knowles, Jr., who have given valuable help in many ways, and to the secretaries of the English Department at North Carolina State College, who have assisted in the typing.

I am grateful to the committee of the Faculty Research and Professional Development Fund of North Carolina State Col-

lege and to the Ford Foundation for generous support in the
publication of this study.

LODWICK HARTLEY

February, 1960   North Carolina State College

CONTENTS

Page

COWPER'S LIFE AND WORKS

I

THE LITERARY REPUTATION: A PREFATORY SURVEY

A WELL-KNOWN SCHOLAR and teacher has been known to remark that since everybody understands Burns, Burns does
not need to be taught, and since nobody understands Blake,
Blake cannot be taught; therefore, for the purposes of any
course in eighteenth-century English literature, William Cowper is obliged to be the most important poet between 1775 and
1800. And in a recent survey of literary scholarship, Professor
James L. Clifford has said: "If Blake and Burns are excluded
. . . as being essentially in the romantic tradition, then the
major poet of the late eighteenth century is William Cowper."[12]
Indeed, a kind of victory by default seems close to becoming an
established assumption in evaluating the quiet man of Olney.

Burns's lyric appeal has become as permanent as Sappho's
or Heinrich Heine's; and Blake's fascination as poet and painter
has undergone a steady growth. Clearly, Cowper's appeal must
be on quite a different basis from that of these two contemporaries—both of whom, incidentally, admired him as a poet.
Burns, in fact, thought him to be "the best poet out of sight
since Thomson," regarding *The Task* as "a glorious poem";[428]
and Blake, coupling aesthetic appreciation of Cowper's phys-
iognomy with a critical appreciation of his literary achievement, wrote to Hayley in 1804: "I have the happiness of seeing
the Divine countenance in such men as Cowper and Milton
more distinctly than in any prince or hero."[438]

Cowper's reputation among the periodical critics of his own day has been treated elsewhere[348] and need not concern us here in detail. It will be sufficient to say at present that neither the mixed reception of the 1782 volume nor the enthusiastic critical response to *The Task* reflects the complete quality or extent of the poet's contemporary appeal among both the literary figures of the time and the relatively unlettered.

However, although Cowper won the warm esteem of such contemporaries as Burns and Blake, he did not always fare equally well among the writers immediately succeeding. The young Wordsworth read him with admiration and sympathy, at one point copying "Yardley Oak" in a notebook for later use in "Yew-Trees."[440] In conversation Coleridge acknowledged him to be "the best of modern poets" and the founder of a new school; and Southey became his first really competent biographer and editor. But actually the poet of Olney did not bulk large in the minds of the Lakists, who were too busy blazing trails of their own to pay a great deal of attention to pioneering that had gone on earlier in Buckinghamshire. The unfavorable reference in the preface to *Lyrical Ballads* is well known. Leigh Hunt's wry remark may reflect quite accurately what happened to Cowper's reputation even among those Romanticists who were early attracted to him. "He was alone," Hunt asserted, "not because he led the way, but because he was left on the roadside."[352]

To Keats, inspired as he was by Spenser's *Faerie Queene* and Chapman's translation of Homer, Cowper offered no "realms of gold"; and a young atheist and revolutionary like Shelley could hardly have been attracted by Cowper's piety or have thought his passion for freedom little more than routine Whiggism. Byron might understandably have been annoyed because by contrast Cowper's "angelic" note had at times been used to deprecate his "satanic" one. Clearly he found it difficult to speak of the bard of Olney with anything but contempt. "That maniacal Calvinist and coddled poet," Byron called him when he acknowledged Cowper to be a poet at all. The noble lord was more inclined to assert flatly that Cowper was "no poet," softening the harshness of the judgment only by adding that "he was a good man and lived at a fortunate time for his works." It is true, nevertheless, that upon occasion he found it convenient to quote Cowper and perhaps in the "Sonnet on Chillon" and "The Prisoner of Chillon" even to borrow something from Cowper's portrayal of the victim of the Bastille in *The Task*. Some of Byron's contempt is reflected in the assertion of James Smith, a co-author of *Rejected Addresses*, in the *London Review* in 1809, accusing the biographer Hayley of trying to make his "mole-hill Cowper over-top Mount Milton."

Charles Lamb, whose own suffering gave him a genuine basis of sympathy with Cowper, always had an affectionate bias toward the poet, especially delighting in his "divine chit-chat"—an epithet that both he and Coleridge were pleased to use. Although Hazlitt took vigorous issue with Byron for speaking as disparagingly as he did of Cowper's talents, he himself was to do the poet no great service by insisting that "there is an effeminacy about him, which shrinks from and repels hearty and common sympathy."

The impression of effeminacy was naturally perpetuated by the fact that so much of his literary reputation was ordered by women—just as such ladies as Mrs. Unwin, Lady Austen, and Lady Hesketh ordered his life. It is significant that Jane Austen allowed Marianne Dashwood in *Sense and Sensibility* to use Cowper's poetry for testing the sensibility of her sister's suitor. Hannah More's undermining of his manhood was even more drastic in what she intended to be entirely enthusiastic and generous appraisal: "I have found what I have been looking for all my life, a poet whom I can read on a Sunday, and whose whole writings I can recommend to my young and my female friends, without restriction or exception."

In the drab rectory at Haworth, the depressed and despondent Brontës read "The Castaway" avidly. Both Charlotte and

Emily, one critic suggests, adopted a castaway as the hero or
heroine of their first novels. In *Shirley*, in which Charlotte has
Caroline Helstone quote the poem to the heroine, Shirley Keel-
dar, the following dialogue ensues:

> "I hope William Cowper is safe and calm in heaven
> now," said Caroline.
> "Do you pity what he suffered on earth?" asked Miss
> Keeldar.
> "Pity him, Shirley? What can I do else? He was
> nearly broken-hearted when he wrote that poem, and it
> almost breaks one's heart to read it. But he found re-
> lief in writing it—I know he did; and that gift of poetry
> —the most divine bestowed on man—was, I believe,
> granted to allay emotions when their strength threatens
> harm. It seems to me, Shirley, that nobody should write
> poetry to exhibit intellect or attainment. Who cares for
> that sort of poetry? Who cares for learning—who cares
> for fine words in poetry? And who does not care for
> feeling—real feeling—however simply, even rudely ex-
> pressed?"

Anne Brontë, who had been unable to free herself from the
bonds of Calvinism, dedicated some verses to Cowper written,
as Abbé Dimnet put it, "as between comrades in misfortune."
Maria Edgeworth read him with sympathy. Later in the
century Mrs. Browning was moved by the poet's sad story to
write some sentimental lines, provoking Oliver Elton's just
remark that "Mrs. Browning's verses on his grave show less
self-control than any of Cowper's own"; and Jane Welsh
Carlyle found that her pity for the poet often took precedence
over her admiration.

George Eliot, it should be said, had a genuine admiration for
Cowper, apart from any sentimentality that may customarily
have been attached to him. Even for the hymns, she had a
finely sensitive appreciation. "Do you remember Cowper's

Hymn beginning 'I was a grovelling creature once,' " she wrote to Maria Lewis on July 21, 1841. "It is lovely and rich as the pomegranate and [*sic*] the vine."

Only the "Swan of Litchfield," Miss Anna Seward, may be cited as an evidence of at least partial resistance among the highly literate ladies of two centuries. Though she consistently objected to the way in which Cowper "demonised the Deity," she did share with her friend John Savile the "delicious" flavor of *The Task*. Yet she felt that no "colossal claim" could be made for the muse of Cowper, though destined "to immortal remembrance"; and she ranked above him her friend Dr. Erasmus Darwin—who, incidentally, had no excessively high regard for Cowper either, and thus did not attempt to challenge the judgment.

Doubtless, both Byron's idea that the poet lived at a fortunate time for his works and Miss More's corollary that he could be safely read by any lady even on Sunday serve to explain his great popularity, quite apart from critical praise or blame by his contemporaries or by the immediately succeeding generations. The surge of the Evangelical Revival plainly created an audience for him that he could hardly have had if he had written at any other time. And the sad facts of his life—not at the very first, but soon inseparably coupled with his poetry and his letters—gave his works an aura of sensibility that, while a deterrent to a completely fair appraisal of the man and his literary achievement, could not have failed to stimulate the sale of his books.

Whatever may have been his reputation, his tremendous popularity at the end of the eighteenth and well into the nineteenth century is demonstrable in publication data. Henry Crabb Robinson stated that Cowper's poetry netted for Joseph Johnson, the publisher, the sum of £10,000, a considerable amount for the time.[712] Even more impressive is Mrs. Norma H. Russell's listing (in a forthcoming bibliography) of over ninety collected editions of Cowper's verse from 1782 to 1837—exclusive of American editions of which there were many.

The story of Cowper's popularity in America in several ways parallels that of his popularity in his homeland. Soon after the success of *The Task* in England, American editions began appearing, to continue throughout the first half of the ensuing century. Even before such editions began to appear, Benjamin Franklin, as an old man, read and enjoyed a gift copy of the 1782 volume of the *Poems*; thus he has the distinction of being the first distinguished American to express enthusiastic appreciation of the poet. Timothy Dwight in "Greenfield Hill" (1794) was among the first of the American imitators. V. L. Parrington found echoes of Cowper's verse in the poetry of young Philadelphians around 1800;[439] and R. L. Rusk has recorded evidences of the early penetration of Cowper's works even into backwoods America, citing the facts that copies of the *Olney Hymns* were available at a Lexington, Kentucky, store as early as 1793 and that lines from *The Task* were printed in *The Palladium* of Frankfort in the same state on August 9, 1798.[1021]

At the end of the colonial period, the most characteristic books to be found in the homes of literate New Englanders were Milton, Bunyan, and Cowper. Many of the important literary figures in the East either read Cowper in their childhood and youth or had the poet read to them. Mrs. Longfellow, for example, read Cowper, Hannah More, and Ossian to her children. Emerson early read Cowper with relish and quoted him in his boyhood letters. His advice to Hannah Haskins Ladd, probably in 1824, is significant, not only for his opinion of the poet, but also for the indication that it gives of the general reading public to which Cowper might be expected to appeal: "If you love poetry make acquaintance with Milton Pope and Cowper, and if you love romance you may read Scott's Novels without sin or scandal." Both Bryant and Whittier also encountered the poet when they were quite young. Bryant has been pictured as reading him sprawled on the floor, his only light a birchwood fire. He was also said to be able to commit pages of *The Task* to memory. He could not rank the poet Young with Cowper, he later wrote,"for he had not the same delicate perception of beauty, the same sense of symmetry and proportion, and the same affectionate observation of nature." Thus he established his basic criteria of appreciation. Whittier recorded his early sympathetic response especially to "the lyric sweep and pathos" of "On the Loss of the Royal George" and his acquaintance with the rest of the poetry is well established. Both of these poets were eventually considered to be American counterparts of Cowper. Lowell's comment on Bryant in the *Fable for Critics* is quite familiar:

He's a Cowper condensed, with no craziness bitten,
And the advantage that Wordsworth before him had
    written.

In "The Snow-Messengers" Paul Hamilton Hayne pictured Whittier as retired and tranquil, sitting by the hearth, taking delight in his cat and dog, yet able to lash out when "wrong threats the public weal"—

God's innocent pensioners in the woodlands dim,
The fields and pastures, know and trust in him;
And in *their* love his lonely heart is blessed,
Our pure, hale-minded Cowper of the West!

Hayne's implied admiration for Cowper's strength of utterance is as interesting and important as is the indication of the poet's influence. Lowell had not been so flattering, obliquely expressing his opinion that Cowper was no "giant," as Wordsworth plainly was. In his amusing note on the pronunciation of Cowper's name, however, Lowell implies that public opinion might be otherwise:

To demonstrate quickly and easily how per-
    versely absurd 'tis to sound this name *Cowper*,

As people in general call him named *super*,
I think that he rhymes it himself with horse-trooper.

Before the middle of the century, adverse criticism of Wordsworth in American periodicals was often coupled with a comparison favorable to Cowper.[1014] Thus a critic in the *North American Review* in 1832 asserted that if Wordsworth had not "entangled himself in an unlucky theory" (that of the preface to *Lyrical Ballads*), he might have had the "tavern popularity" of Cowper, Burns, and Scott. In 1847 a writer in the same review, castigating followers of Wordsworth who had carried the "worship of nature to a ridiculous excess," asserted, "If this disorder had not passed the use of medicine, we would counsel them to go and study Cowper's *Task*, and to be ashamed of their mystic ravings and transcendental silliness."

It is just as understandable that Cowper had a limited appeal for Poe as it is that he had none for Byron. Although, like Byron, Poe on occasion quoted Cowper, he regarded the English poet as belonging to "an era of criticism" rather than to a more vigorous "era of impulse." To a later brooding genius like Herman Melville, on the other hand, Cowper had a particular appeal because he symbolized wisdom that came through suffering.

Thus in America as in England one may detect various levels and kinds of reactions to the poet. Clearly, his piety, his fresh and individual delineations of nature, his pleas for the oppressed, and his mental torture were elements of his appeal. At least some of these might also be repulsive. Lowell's observation concerning "C.'s penchant to preach" is typical of the negative kind of reaction to Cowper that has appeared in many places and at many times. But, it must be remembered, there were many less highly sophisticated people to whom his sort of Evangelical sermonizing was appealing. And, again, the real index to the poet's popularity in America, as in England, was not what critics said about him but how many people bought his books.

As far as English periodical critics were concerned, the high regard in which Cowper was held in some quarters in the first half of the nineteenth century is clearly indicated in Christopher North's retrospective pronouncement in *Blackwood's Magazine* for February, 1832: "The era has been glorious—that includes Cowper and Wordsworth, Burns and Byron." At this time there could be little doubt that Cowper's general popularity was markedly vigorous as evidenced by publishing activity involving both his works and his biography. The rivalry of Grimshawe and Southey in getting out a biography and a complete edition of the works was soon to develop. In 1849, on the other hand, as Charles Ryskamp has recently pointed out, Lord Carlisle recorded how dinner conversation of "The Club" involved Cowper's being "talked of as having been called the most popular of English poets" and how at the time some doubts were cast as to whether "he still holds that position." Participating in the discussion were Lord Lansdowne, Lord Ellesmere, Henry Hallam, and Thomas Babington Macaulay, among others.

Could this occasion be taken as a sort of climax of Cowper's literary reputation and his popularity in England? Such a conclusion would be debatable. For years to come editions of Cowper's poetry kept issuing from the presses. Many were beautiful and ornate, with fine steel engravings, tooled leather bindings, and gilt lettering and edging—all in the most elegant Victorian tradition of bookmaking. Furthermore, Sainte-Beuve in France had yet to express his delight in Cowper and to acclaim his *poésie domestique*, an opinion that could scarcely have gone unnoticed across the Channel in England. And one of the most formidable voices in all English criticism—namely that of Matthew Arnold—was still to include Cowper's name in a limited list of "our chief poetical names"—even though, it is true, this inclusion called forth a modicum of unfavorable comparison of Cowper with some of the Elizabethan poets whom Arnold had not elected to recognize. Tennyson, too, admired his poetic gifts.[819]

Other Victorian and Edwardian critics, intelligent though they were in their estimates, might be accused of "coddling." Yet one cannot discount the delight and enthusiasm of Walter Bagehot, Austin Dobson, and Augustine Birrell. Critics like Sir Leslie Stephen, the Reverend Stopford Brooke, and Edward Dowden did more than some of their contemporaries in emphasizing the serious elements of Cowper's thought and poetry in contrast to the "divine chit-chat" that had become established as perennially charming in the letters and, to some extent, in the poetry. Twentieth-century writers of such stature as Virginia Woolf and E. M. Forster have found Cowper worth reading.

Yet looking back from the mid-point of the twentieth century, one might conclude—without careful examination of all the evidence—that from 1895 to the present Cowper had undergone a drastic decline both in popularity and in reputation. No longer are fine editions of his works coming from the press; no longer is he a "school classic," as he was in England and in America at least through the first decades of the present century; and textbooks on "major" British writers frequently omit him.

The impression of a marked decline in interest might seem to be bolstered by Randall Jarrell's recent novel, *Pictures from an Institution*, satirically depicting an English Department head in an Eastern college whose specialty is Cowper and whose besetting frustration is the fact that, because of the similarity in the pronunciation of the names, everybody confuses his man with James Fenimore Cooper.[1010] When the "Head" attempts to explain, "most of the world wasn't there to explain to; people cared little for Cooper, but less for Cowper." Further along, the novelist observes concerning an engraving of the poet hanging above the mantel in the harassed scholar's house: "The stocking-cap on the poet's head, the tea cup in the poet's hand had to him a look of limitation, of almost feminine restraint. Cowper's life seemed to him a sheltered one: it did no good to remind himself that Cowper had been for a good deal of his life, insane."

If this fictional projection is palpably false in regard to any extant portrait of Cowper, it is for any careful student false to the same extent in its implications. On the other hand, Jarrell's own inaccuracies are ironical evidences of some general truth in his position.

Especially in America, one may have to admit, Cowper in the mid-twentieth century is no longer well known by either that nebulous character called the "average reader" or even by all students of English literature, in spite of the fact that at least five of his hymns are sung regularly in Protestant churches throughout the English-speaking world, that "John Gilpin" is still read with delight by many, and that such expressions as "variety's the very spice of life" and "God moves in a mysterious way" are frequently encountered clichés. In this last regard, it is interesting to note that the latest edition of the *Oxford Dictionary of Quotations* still accords Cowper equal space with Pope as one of the most frequently quoted poets in the language; and the twelfth edition of Bartlett's *Familiar Quotations*, though giving Pope over twice as many columns, continues to allow Cowper much more space than Gray, Blake, or Burns—though not so much as Goldsmith.

As far as students of English literature are concerned, the vogue of Pope and the Augustans on one side and the towering witness of Wordsworth's importance on the other may have tended to overshadow Cowper. Evidence of something short of enthusiasm among scholars appears in the late Donald Stauffer's statement that "Cowper's *The Task* is well named for the long stretches that present rural and domestic life in all its fragments."[719] Sir Herbert Grierson, with warm sympathy for Burns, sees Cowper "first and foremost" as "an Evangelical preacher."[342] And George Sherburn, an eminent Pope scholar, in his rather routine treatment of Cowper in a recent history of English literature sums up the tone of his whole attitude toward the poet of Olney by saying that his verse is "like his favorite beverage, at best cheering, never inebriating."[305]

There can also be little argument that twentieth-century literary criticism in the university quarterlies, in the "little" magazines, and in the sophisticated "slicks" has virtually ignored Cowper. Edmund Wilson, in a passing reference in *The New Yorker*, could say merely that his verse was "only a little above mediocrity."[321] Actually, as one may easily guess, Cowper is neglected by the main body of contemporary critics because his poetry seemingly gives them so little to go on. One may study his imagery, but not for long. The search for paradox, irony, symbolism, and ambiguity in his verse offers no great excitement. Only in a lyric like "The Castaway" and in a handful of other isolated pieces does the critic find material for extended explication. Most of Cowper's poetry, in short, is uni-vocal, demanding understanding on only one level. What appeal, therefore, could it have to T. S. Eliot or William Empson or Kenneth Burke?

It may have been with some justification then that Donald Davie recently exclaimed, "After Ben Jonson, Cowper is the most neglected of our poets."[324] On the other hand, the bibliography appended to this essay offers extensive evidence to the contrary. It will demonstrate that in certain quarters interest has been vigorous. And even in its least favorable aspect, it will argue that Cowper has, in a Faulknerian sense, "endured."

Indeed, no one need expect a rediscovery or a revival of Cowper, like the twentieth-century revival of his putative ancestor, John Donne. The Cowper Society will never function with the enthusiasm and vigor of the Johnsonians, with convivial and scholarly celebrations of birthdays and other anniversaries. Nor will the readers of Cowper attain the status of devotees that the Janeites assume. But, as Professor Enright has put it, "although [Cowper] is unlikely to enjoy any future vogue, he has something to offer which will never fall entirely out of fashion or out of date."[332] It is on such an assumption that continued interest in him may firmly rest.

II

BIOGRAPHICAL PROBLEMS AND TWENTIETH-CENTURY BIOGRAPHERS

"Cowper's life offers more of an adventure in understanding than his poetry," Hugh I'Anson Fausset contended in at least partial justification of his biographical study.[227] Sir Herbert Grierson has echoed the sentiment in the assertion that "Cowper, the man . . . is of greater interest today than the poems themselves."[342] This position, however, is one with which some contemporary students of Cowper have justly wished to take issue. The neglect of his considerable worth as a poet, they contend, can largely be attributed to an exaggerated emphasis on the sad or on the controversial aspects of his life. On the other hand, it is quite obvious that biographical interest has maintained a remarkable constancy, regardless of fluctuations in critical opinion; moreover, it can be argued that the poet has gained rather than lost readers through the perennial interest in his life. There have always been people who have considered him to be no poet. There have been few who have not found his biography appealing.

Actually from the very beginning, biographical interest in Cowper has flourished under the stimulus of controversy. In view of the fact that the poet lived an outwardly quiet and uneventful life, this circumstance is ironical. Yet the "mild" man of Olney was hardly cold in his grave before seeds of a debate were sown that were to produce an appreciable harvest for over a century after his death.

The result was, in the main, a large number of biographical treatments that were scarcely more than interpretations (or, at times, extended sermons) and that evidenced an appalling absence of anything like an objective approach in the discovery and sifting of facts. Between 1800 and 1900 there were no fewer than thirty such treatments—many of them by clergymen. Some of them were brief, to be sure, and attached to editions of the poetry or the letters. Of all those who undertook the writing of a "life" or a "memoir," only three—Samuel Greatheed, William Hayley, and John Johnson—knew the poet and, therefore, could contribute first-hand material; and, if we omit an editor-biographer like John Bruce, only two—Robert Southey and Thomas Wright—engaged in extensive research.

The early story of the controversy that from its inception effectually precluded objectivity has been told in some detail elsewhere.[232] Nevertheless, since the early established pattern is unmistakably reflected even in the most recent biographical interpretations, it must be briefly treated here.

In May, 1800, two Evangelical friends preached funeral sermons on Cowper: John Newton in London and Samuel Greatheed in Olney.[284] Because the sermon of the latter was the more widely quoted and also because it became the basic source of comment on Cowper in the Evangelical press and the substance of at least two memoirs in book form, it can certainly be regarded as an essential document in the verbal battle over the possible religious causes of the poet's dementia. On the surface, the sermon to a modern reader may not seem to be controversial at all, for it simply takes the position that Cowper had been sensitive from childhood and that he had shown ample signs of a tendency toward madness well before his first contacts with Evangelicalism. Cowper is presented as a "bush which burned and was not consumed" and an attempt is made to "vindicate the ways of God" in the suffering of the poet. But when the sermon appeared in print, the Anglican press reacted quickly and strongly, regarding it as an unjustifiable apology for Evangelical enthusiasm, a "cruel" homily, and "an awful warning against the errors of Methodism."

Two lines of arguments were immediately established: the one contending that the poet's madness stemmed either from natural causes or from sin in some form, original or personal (actual); the other insisting that the abnormal emotionalism and depressing eschatology of Evangelicalism were the poet's undoing. Since Evangelicalism had its own contrasting if not opposing camps, even a third line was to emerge: namely, that Calvinistic not Arminian theology was—if any religious cause could be assigned—the source of the trouble. Because, by his own admission, John Newton's reputation for "preaching people mad" was reasonably widespread, this redoubtable divine early became the villain of the anti-Evangelicals.

By the time William Hayley got out the first two volumes of his life of Cowper in 1803 the pattern of the battle was fixed. The biographer, a minor poet with a big heart, suffered the unhappy fate of an official or authorized biographer in having his hands tied by his subject's strong-willed cousin Lady Hesketh, who insisted that the life should be written like a "novel" and that all references to such matters as the poet's early love affair with Theodora Cowper, his attempts at suicide, and his "devotional excesses" should be curtailed. With the best of intentions to be non-controversial and to please everybody, Hayley pleased neither the Evangelicals nor their detractors. By the former he was accused of deliberately distorting the portrait of his subject by omitting the religious letters and, far worse, by attributing Cowper's madness to religious causes. The anti-Evangelicals attacked him for prolixity and inaccuracy, pointing out the "enthusiastic intolerance" of Cowper's poetry and insisting on Methodism as the cause of the poet's "martyrdom."

Evangelical friends of the poet immediately set about correcting the record. Greatheed wrote a "Memoir" in the April and May issues of the *Evangelical Magazine* in 1803, and a

little volume based on it was rushed from the press in the same
year, ostensibly to supplement Hayley for "the religious mind"
and to erect a defense of Newton in particular and Evangelicalism in general. Its thesis was suggested in a poem by the
Reverend T. Beck appended to the "revised" and "corrected"
1814 edition:

> Religion never gave the wound
> Which Cowper felt within;
> 'Twas in corrupted nature found,
> Th' effect of Adam's sin.

It was not until 1824 that Cowper's kinsman, John Johnson,
supplied many of the letters that Hayley had omitted. Once
this was done Hayley and Johnson were fair game for the
biographers who wished to use them. Thus Thomas Taylor in
the preface to his pro-Evangelical *Life* of 1832 accurately
designates his work a "compilation" from Hayley and Johnson
containing "remarks" on the poet's "writings and on the
peculiarities of his interesting character never before published." Other biographers were not always so completely
ingenuous. And not all—it should be said—were entirely so
reliant on the previously published sources. As a reasonably
rare example of independence, John Bruce in preparing his
memoir for the Aldine edition of the poetry in 1830 did valuable
spadework in materials outside the easily accessible published
ones. In interesting contrast to Taylor's Evangelical apologetics, Bruce takes the position that Newton fostered Cowper's
"mental infirmity"; at the same time he tactfully dwells as
little as possible on the poet's overhanging "calamity."

If Hayley was dogged by difficulties from Cowper's family,
Southey had difficulties which, though of a different sort, had
some relationship to the same problem. Approached in 1833 to
do a biography and a complete edition of the works, Southey
accepted, with the assumption that his publisher could obtain
the rights to John Johnson's edition of the *Private Correspond-*

ence. Johnson's publishers delayed, in the meantime quietly engaging Johnson's brother-in-law, the Reverend Thomas Grimshawe, to execute a biography and an edition similar to the one projected by Southey's publishers. Thus Southey found himself not only cut off from the full use of the valuable letters but also presented with a rival in the field. Since he could not print the correspondence, he had to resort to the dodge of attempting to weave it into his narrative. This procedure naturally made his original biography long and tedious. After the copyright on the edition of the letters finally ran out, the correspondence was removed to the end of the biography as a supplement. But the damage was already done. Clearly, Southey's respect for Evangelicalism could not have been enhanced by what had happened. At any rate, his biography expresses the prejudice of the Anglican rank and file against religious enthusiasm, showing antipathy toward Newton and giving considerable weight to the theory that religion played a significant part in Cowper's madness. Though Southey's biography may be in Fausset's phrase "too sententiously and ecclesiastically moral" and in Goldwin Smith's "too prolix and too much filled out with dissertations for the common reader," it remains a remarkably rich treatment, not yet completely superseded by anything that has come after it.

Of the numerous biographers between Southey and Thomas Wright, few contribute significant factual materials or make important changes in the pattern of interpretation. One may cite as typical the memoir of Charles Whitehead attached to an edition of the *Poetical Works* in 1849. Frankly based on Greatheed, Hayley, Johnson, and Southey, it occasionally takes issue with its sources—notably Hayley, who unhappily became a whipping boy—but it is quite devoid of anything new. Its overemphasis on Cowper's last years leads up to a homiletic moral that might easily have been lifted directly out of Greatheed: ". . . if it was the Almighty's will to chasten so strictly such a man as Cowper, how thankful ought we to be for every blessing that attends, and how patient and resigned under every calamity that befals [sic] us." Less obviously derivative and less biased is Robert Bell's brief memoir attached to his edition of the poetry in 1854. Illustrative of the kind of editorial heat that continued to be generated by the anti-Newtonians is a statement contained in the short "life" by J. M. Ross prefacing *Poems by William Cowper* published in Edinburgh by William P. Nimmo in 1863: "One's indignation grows hot to see how callously the *Newtonites* (if we may so designate the 'righteous overmuch' friends of the poet who have handled this point of his life) speak of his ruined peace and health; and how fervidly, on the other hand, they describe his transports of feverish devotion." An echo of Burns's reaction to the "unco guid" is apparent.

Canon William Benham's memoir prefixed to the still valuable Globe Edition, first issued in 1870, is compact and scholarly, with a useful critical treatment of the poetry.[106] Toward Evangelicalism, however, Benham found it impossible to maintain complete objectivity:

> I do not believe certainly that religious opinions were the original cause of the madness. When I began the study of this life I believed that I should find that the views were merely the form which the madness happened to take. But this belief I cannot now hold. It became as clear to me as any demonstration could make it, that the Calvinistic doctrine and religious excitements threw an already trembling mind off its balance, and aggravated a malady which but for them might probably have been cured.

Goldwin Smith, on the other hand, wrote his slight essay in the English Men of Letters Series in 1880 without any of Benham's distrust of religious enthusiasm. Though he may have fallen short of discerning the complexities of Cowper's malady (calling it "simple hypochondria" resulting from "delicacy of constitution and weakness of digestion"), he is able to see that if Cowper's "hypochondria took a religious form . . . so did his recovery" and that "both must be set down to the account of his faith, or neither." He firmly absolves Newton of Calvinism that was "very dark or sulphureous," and he everywhere treats Evangelicalism as a constructive rather than a destructive force in the poet's life, capable of bringing him both happiness and inspiration.

This position is close to one that had already been expressed by Whitwell Elwin in a *Quarterly Review* article in 1860, which Elwin later attempted to expand into a full-length biography and which was published posthumously in an unfinished state in 1902.[224] In staunch refusal to allow Cowper's religion to be blamed for his madness, Elwin pointed out that heredity could well have played a significant part, since the poet's uncle Ashley Cowper had been known to have attacks of melancholia and since Ashley's second daughter Theodora "lived to exhibit eccentricities inconsistent with sanity." His theory that the primary cause of the mental state was a "weakly constitution" which had as a "basis or accompaniment deranged digestive functions" exactly coincides with Smith's.

By 1892 when Thomas Wright brought out the first edition of his *Life*, a re-examination of the original documents, together with a recompilation of the material that had been accumulating throughout the century, was long overdue. Since Wright lived in Olney, he naturally had the advantage of immediate access to much local material not available to his predecessors. What he executed was undeniably a labor of love. If the result was not merely "little more than a catalogue of events," as Fausset has ungraciously designated it, yet even in the greatly improved revised edition it falls short of the kind of definitive biographical treatment that important figures of English literature were beginning to receive. Wright's generally gentle tone is well revealed in his indirect disclaimer of any religious bias:

This is not the place to discuss the merits or demerits of the Evangelicals. Their preaching would scarcely suit the present day. But they do not live in the present day. They were good and earnest men, they lived according to their lights, and they ought to be held in honour by every section of the church.

Between the first edition of Wright's *Life* in 1892 and the second edition in 1921, there was a noticeable hiatus in biographical effort, broken effectively only by Sir James G. Frazer's astute and competent biographical essay prefacing his edition of the *Letters*.[121] This does not, of course, account for the flurry of interest in both biographical and critical matters occasioned by the centennial of Cowper's death in 1900. Nor does it include random periodical essays such as Alice Law's scarcely illuminating consideration of "the vexed question of Newton's influence,"[241] Herbert J. Norman's summary of the various reasons assigned to the poet's madness,[251] an unpublished doctoral dissertation with biographical emphasis like that of Neilson C. Hannay at Harvard University,[231] or several other publications by members of the Cowper Society that include useful subsidiary materials.[218]

A substantial revival in biographical interest was heralded by Gamaliel Bradford's essay "Diversions of a Lost Soul" published in the *Atlantic Monthly* in 1924.[206] Applying the method of "psychography" and maintaining a steady emphasis on Cowper's preoccupation with the idea of his own damnation, Bradford prepared the way both for the reopening of the old controversy and for the application of modern psychological methods to the appraisal of Cowper's mental state—though the author contributes nothing else of real significance.

The essay leads up to Hugh I'Anson Fausset's *William Cowper* of 1928,[227] a work that mounts so vigorous an attack on Evangelical religion that one may at times wonder whether to regard it first as interpretation or as polemic. Of Evangeli-

calism, Fausset asserts, "Its God was but little removed from
the Jehovah whose mouth watered at the smell of charred
cattle, and was less true to the facts of life than impartial
Nemesis treading upon the heels of Hubris. Its dogma was
adapted only to primitive natures . . . " Newton, the argument
runs, endowed God with his own ruthlessness and for a time
succeeded in inducing Cowper to sacrifice his intelligence on
this God's grisly altar. Fausset concludes:

> And it was Evangelicalism which, by compelling him
> to abase his reason and his free-will before an omnipotent
> Providence, made him a necessitarian, converting an in-
> nate timidity and one sadly aggravated by early cir-
> cumstance into a fixed delusion of unpardonable sin.

As a poet, Fausset feels, Cowper should have realized that
he had a duty to transcend dogmatic religion. This he might
have done if he had had the courage to "give himself passionately to life." But, as the case was, he was caught in a tension
between poetry and religion; and both Cowper and poetry were
the victims.

As a critical study of the poet's genius the work is everywhere vigorous rather than judicious. Its wrong-headedness
has, as one would expect, not gone unnoticed. Nevertheless,
its tendency to stimulate strong reaction and to provoke a re-
examination of Cowper's biography and his poetry has made it
valuable.

Lord David Cecil's *The Stricken Deer*[215] in the following year
is a book that admittedly grew out of a desire to retell the story
of an intriguing character rather than to undertake the more
onerous pursuit of fresh material or to engage in controversy.
Equipped with fine sensitivity, a confident knowledge of the
eighteenth-century background, and an exceptionally attractive prose style, Lord David achieved a piece of literary
portraiture that was a popular success and that is still regarded
as a minor classic. In it Cowper becomes a charming period

piece in a presentation that would have appealed to Charles
Lamb or Austin Dobson. But the biography is essentially a
refined piece of "coddling," hardly satisfactory as more than
entertainment to anyone who has any real acquaintance with
the genuine elements of seriousness and strength in the poet's
character and work.

With the basic religious controversy, Lord David is not
deeply involved. Cowper's tragedy, as he sees it, was not that
Evangelicalism failed to heal him but that nothing else could.
Evangelical religion, he acknowledges, was at first a blessing to
the poet, who needed a warmer faith than the latitudinarian
Establishment of his day could offer. Yet his innate sensibility
and refinement made the crudity of the new movement impossible to accept completely. In short, this position comes
dangerously near assuming that Cowper was too much of a
gentleman ever really to become a Methodist.

A more direct answer to Fausset came in 1935 in Gilbert
Thomas' *William Cowper and the Eighteenth Century*, which is
unabashedly Methodist in sympathy.[280] Insisting that the poet
cannot be understood apart from the Evangelical revival,
Thomas sets about to refute the "common impression" (found
specifically in Frazer, Fausset, and in Lord David Cecil) that
Cowper's insanity was "needlessly aggravated, if not actually
caused by Evangelicalism . . . whose evil angel was . . . John
Newton." His own view of Cowper's malady is a return to the
view of Goldwin Smith, Whitwell Elwin, and Clement Shorter
that the mental disease was constitutional and that Newton is
to be exonerated. Not only was the influence of Newton
"relatively innocuous," he argues; it was on the whole "broadening and beneficent." Thomas also argues against the frequent exaggeration of Cowper's insanity. The poet, he points
out with justice, was not only for the greater part of his life
quite sane but he was also at times "quintessentially sane."
Thomas gives credit to Goldwin Smith (though it should go to a
much earlier biographer) for first making the distinction be-

tween the Calvinistic and the Arminian elements in Cowper's thinking. Cowper's story might have been different, Thomas believes, if his thought had been more definitely influenced by the softness of Arminianism than by the severity of Calvinism: "Calvinism intensified (though it did not cause) his morbidity; Arminianism warmed his heart."

Two studies of 1942 and 1943 expanded upon the religious debate. Writing in the *Philological Quarterly* on "The Religion of John Newton," Adelaide Thein found the faith of her subject to be far less "mild" and "relatively innocuous" than Thomas had concluded.[277] Her position actually becomes a return to at least part of Fausset's. On the other hand, in a study of "Cowper and the Unpardonable Sin" in the *Journal of Religion* Maurice Quinlan concluded that the poet's conviction of damnation could have stemmed neither from the Calvinistic nor from the Arminian theology of his day.[259] He further vindicated Newton by arguing that, though his theological bias was admittedly more Calvinistic than Arminian, Cowper's own Calvinism was more pronounced than Newton's.

In a later and more fully argued doctoral dissertation, Miss Thein contends that Cowper's obsession and his considered beliefs were quite separate—one arising from his neurosis, the other from "fairly unified sources of reason and feeling."[278] Cowper, she further asserts, rejected the fundamental doctrines of both the Arminians and the Calvinists—the soft and vain perfectionism of the Wesleyans and the harsh "unrighteous" fatalism of the most rabid in either camp of Evangelicalism— ultimately arriving at a high social and ethical creed "like Anglicanism at its best."

As important as the subject of Cowper's dementia has been, the discussion of its origin (as I have already suggested) has been pursued in the main by religious controversialists and amateur psychologists or psychiatrists rather than by scientifically equipped students. Even leaving the religious aspects aside, early causes advanced ranged widely from a contemporary rumor (apparently reported by the Reverend David Simpson, curate to Cowper's friend, William Unwin) that the poet's first derangement was caused by his rejection by the kept mistress of Lord Thurlow[235] to the reason suggested in the unexpurgated version of the *Greville Memoirs* that his mental state stemmed from a concealed physical defect: "He was an Hermaphrodite; somebody knew his secret, and probably threatened his exposure."[230] Other later conjectures involving physical causes have included such things as defective nerve tissue and (as we have seen) malfunctioning of the digestive system.

Whereas these conjectures have been made by non-professionals in the science of diagnosis, there have also been sporadic comments by medical men, though the light that they have shed has not always been more significant than that provided by the amateurs.

It is interesting to note that Cowper was very early the subject of study by an important scientific mind—that of Dr. Benjamin Rush, surgeon in the Continental Army, signer of the Declaration of Independence, professor of medicine at the University of Pennsylvania, and "father of American psychiatry." In 1812, Rush included the case of Cowper—along with that of Dr. Samuel Johnson—in a pioneering work called *Medical Inquiries and Observations upon Diseases of the Mind,* carefully observing the symptoms of the poet's malady and the devices used to allay it. Thus if Dr. Franklin was the first great American and "Citizen of the World" to appreciate the poetry of Cowper, Dr. Rush—who was also a Philadelphian and a friend of the older man—was not only the first American but also the first competent medical man to inquire objectively into Cowper's mental distress.

It was not until a century later, however, that the same kind of interest was shown by another physician. In 1913 Dr. Jean Boutin published in France a "medico-psychological" monograph on the poet.[295] This study is largely a straightforward biographical account with concluding pages devoted to an attempt to describe Cowper's illness from a medical and psychiatric point of view. Boutin's study of the letters, poems, and biographical facts led him to the conclusion that the poet was a melancholiac whose madness was confined to his religious ideas: "Son esprit n'a perdu le contrôle que des faits qui se rattachent à la religion." From melancholy aggravated by delusions of persecution, auditory hallucinations, and suicidal tendencies, the study argues, Cowper turned after the attack of 1773 to poetry as the most effective therapy.

Boutin assigns psychological causes to some of the breakdowns: that of 1763, for example, was caused by Cowper's abnormal fear of appearing in public, that of 1773 by the harmful influence of Newton and his excessive dwelling on damnation, and that near the end of his life by Mrs. Unwin's death. But he also believes that there was a probable underlying organic cause of which the psychological factors were largely surface manifestations. This organic cause (he infers from Cowper's description of various symptoms) was a chronic nephritis, probably among the sequelae of Cowper's early smallpox. The nephritis gave rise to a uraemia with a toxic effect on his system. The three breakdowns might thus have been coincident with the periods in which Cowper's uraemia had increased the toxicity in his system to an intolerable point.

Since Boutin's medico-psychological study, Dr. James H. Lloyd has made a less ambitious examination of Cowper's "circular insanity" (based, incidentally, on inadequate bibliographical sources);[298] and Dr. A. J. Rosanoff has used the poet in his standard *Manual of Psychiatry and Mental Hygiene* as a classic example of the "so-called manic-depressive psychosis."[299]

In a Harvard University dissertation of 1951, H. K. Gregory applies the methods of Freud and his school to a study of the five psychotic derangements of the poet.[297] He examines with some care the Oedipal phase of Cowper's development, noting his "intensely ambivalent feelings" toward his father and his over-idealization of his mother. He considers the possible effect of a genital deformity—postulating a condition known as hypospadias, at times mistaken for hermaphroditism—as a reason for the school bully's early success in tyrannizing over Cowper as well as for Cowper's later abnormal dread of public interrogation before the House of Lords. Gregory also explores the unresolved childhood conflicts that caused the poet to walk a narrow path between man and woman, a kind of "latent homosexuality" manifested in his conflicting horror of femininity on the one hand and masculine aggressiveness on the other. Poetry like his other hobbies, Gregory feels, provided an illusion of mastery over his environment and an escape from the intensity of his conflicts, not a means of resolving them. Thus, it is psychoanalytically—the study concludes—that one can best account for the lack of integration in Cowper's literary production as a whole.

Fully cognizant that the religious argument had gone around and around (Anglicans and other anti-Evangelicals blaming Evangelicalism in general, Arminians inclining toward making Calvinism the bugbear, and the Calvinists staunchly sticking to physical causes, Original Sin, and Divine Providence) Maurice Quinlan attempted in 1953 a "critical life" that would give as nearly as possible a balanced picture.[256] In the main, he succeeded. If he did not achieve such a little classic of urbane portraiture as Lord David Cecil's or as impassioned or vivid a study as Fausset's and Thomas', he provided a sound, straightforward narrative, relying on Cowper's own testimony and the best of antecedent scholarship. The book is free of polemic and it presents no sensational thesis. It contains no recriminations against Evangelical religion for victimizing the poet and no brisk defense of any aspect of the movement as a potential but unavailing ameliorative for his suffering. John Newton is accorded a sympathetic appraisal, and Lady Austen is given the generally unromantic characterization previously established by Kenneth Povey.[253] Only once does Quinlan fall into the kind of wishful thinking found in more partisan accounts, Anglican and Methodist in particular. Like Sainte-Beuve whom he echoes, he thinks that Catholicism with its confessional and "its strong consolation for the believer" might have served to restore the poet's peace of mind.

Although the biographer does not achieve an appreciably new portrait of his subject or provide any major illumination of the problems, he contributes intelligent discussion of such matters as the possible sources of Cowper's ideas on the unpardonable sin, his changing concept of this sin, Newton's belief in dreams as a possible influence on Cowper's hallucinations, and the imagery of Cowper's poetry as it reflects his mental disturbances. The treatment of Cowper's malady is generally handled with a great deal of common sense, though the attempt to explore the question of a physical deformity tends toward dubious conjecture.

As a whole, Quinlan's biography is an entirely respectable example of a biographical tradition whose chief weakness—in spite of its surface vigor—is that it has been inbred and parasitical. Indeed, as it should now be more than apparent, so many interpretations, so many considerations of the poet's religious and psychopathic concerns, have been superimposed on a relatively static body of factual material that, as Charles Ryskamp has put it, "the origins of the chains of information and myth have become so obscure that it has become extremely difficult to separate later interpretation from the evidence of Cowper himself, or from that of his contemporaries." Ryskamp's biographical study of 1959 rejects the overworked interpretative tradition for a "facts and problems" approach designed to seek out new primary sources of information and to re-examine directly the older sources.[263] The scope of the work is the first thirty-six years of the poet's life from his birth at Berkhampstead through his distressing departure from the Temple, his "cure" at Dr. Cotton's, and his residence in

Huntingdon. Since Cowper has been chiefly known as he appeared in his later years—often as a pious and psychotic recluse in a provincial village—the new study seeks to bring the total picture of his life into better perspective by showing him as a reasonably normal and worldly young man—a student in one of England's most distinguished public schools who participated in the usual childhood sports and made warm friends among his fellow Westminsters, an indifferent reader of law and a socially inclined young resident of the Temple, and a smartly dressed member of as bright and witty a club as mid-century London could boast.

By no means, of course, has this side of the picture been unknown, but Ryskamp has been able to document it beyond question and to enrich it at several points. The detailed information produced about the poet's school days at Westminster—his living quarters, his school activities, his sports, his friends—as well as the same kind of information about his residence in the Middle and Inner Temple—is an admirable addition to our factual knowledge of the poet. The same kind of objectivity is maintained in regard to less tangible matters—the "problems" of the young Cowper.

The question of insanity in the Cowper blood—suppressed by early biographers out of deference to the family and only sparsely documented by later ones—is again examined, with additional documentation concerning Theadora [thus in the spelling of her own day]—with whom Ryskamp is willing to believe that the young Cowper was genuinely in love. Both consanguinity (the reason first suggested by James Croft) and the pall of hereditary melancholy are the reasons assigned to Ashley Cowper's causing the relationship of the two cousins to be broken off.

In regard to the related matter of Cowper's alleged physical defect, Ryskamp carefully examines the possible provenance of the statement in the *Greville Memoirs*, as well as the possible logical consequences of such a deformity, concluding that

"Cowper's reputed hermaphroditism was a preoccupation resulting from melancholia." In countering both the suggestions of hermaphroditism and latent homosexuality, he adduces a considerable body of evidence pointing toward Cowper's youthful heterosexuality. The complicated circumstances of Cowper's failure to assume the proffered clerkship in the House of Lords is extensively examined in regard to the political involvements of the Cowper family.

The book is a promising first step in the execution of a definitive biography now long overdue. The writing of such a biography still awaits the completion of a reliable edition of the letters.

III

THE POETRY AND THE LETTERS: MODERN CRITICAL OPINION AND LITERARY SCHOLARSHIP

ANY DISCUSSION OF Cowper's poetry, it should now be plain, will very likely reflect what is usually the initial assumption about it: namely, that of all English poetry his is among the most difficult to separate from the life of the poet. The relationship of the poetry and the biography, in fact, has always seemed so close that each has inevitably been used as a gloss on the other; and biographical and critical works have become all but indistinguishable. Naturally, it is not impossible to read some of the poetry *in vacuo* and to consider it on its own merits. Some of the didactic poems may be so read (whether or not one admires them); and also may such a delightful little classic as "John Gilpin," some of the passages of natural description in *The Task*, and a few of the short lyrics, though these cannot always be considered to be securely in such a category. But for a total appreciation of Cowper's work, a knowledge of the biography is clearly indispensable. As one would expect, the poetry and the letters are closely related.

It should not be surprising that studies of Cowper's poetic technique are relatively rare. This does not mean that technical aspects of his poetry—his metrics and architectonics—have not been commented upon. But he has been regarded so long as a charming amateur that systematic analysis of his work has too often seemed pointless. Notice has been taken of his particular use of the couplet and blank verse,[314] and there has been an elaborate structural study of *The Task* concentrating on its use of "slight connection" and the "associational technique."[700]   Attention has also been given to the imagery, but the most ambitious study of this aspect of the poet's work has been used, as I have already indicated, as much to probe his mental state as to illuminate his poetic technique.[518]

Textual problems such as have existed in many other poets are relatively uncomplicated in Cowper's poetry.   (The letters are another matter—to be discussed later.)   In spite of the fact that nineteenth-century editing did not always maintain high standards and that some liberties were taken with Cowper's poems, such editions as those of Southey, Bell, Bruce (the "Aldine" edition), and Benham (the "Globe") were generally accurate and reliable.   Nevertheless, there remained a need for a fresh text produced with more care than nineteenth-century editors had shown.   This need was met in 1905 by two editions: one by J. C. Bailey[104] and another by Humphrey S. (later Sir Humphrey) Milford.[130]   Though the differences between the two editions are not extensive, Bailey and Milford demonstrate an interesting divergence of opinion on textual authority.

A thorough examination of all the editions published during Cowper's lifetime (together, of course, with an examination of the accessible manuscripts and the best of the nineteenth-century editions) led Bailey to decide that the text of the earliest editions should be followed.   He did so, he stated, "because we have plenty of evidence that Cowper corrected the proofs of both his first and second volumes," whereas there is not "the slightest suggestion that he made any corrections for the editions of 1787 or 1788."

Milford was by no means so willing to rely on the proofreading of the poet. The 1782 volume, he argued, has many misprints—"in spite of the list of errata which gives a false air of accuracy to the edition."   The 1786 edition especially "bristles" with errors.   Thus Milford felt that he could only assume carelessness in the proofreading of the earlier editions.

For this reason he was led to base his text on the royal octavo of 1800. Before 1801, Milford pointed out, there were eleven editions of each of the two separate volumes of 1782 and 1785. These editions he divided into two groups: those from 1782 (1785) to 1788 in the first, the remainder in the second. The second group, he explained, differs from the first in slightly more consistent spelling and in less haphazard punctuation—changes, he admitted, that may never have been definitely adopted either by Cowper or his friends. Nevertheless, he concluded that there is no evidence of Cowper's having objected to the new style of which he was certainly aware. The revised spelling prevented the editor from being "compelled to give the text an American air with 'favor,' 'honor,' 'labor,' &c" and allowed him generally to observe the elision of the "e" in preterite forms, a practice that Cowper favored but in which he was not consistent. The revised punctuation, Milford argued, tends to improve the sense and the rhythm both in the couplets and in the blank verse.

Milford printed the major poems from the 1782 volume, *The Task*, and *Tirocinium* in the order named; these he followed with the miscellaneous poems early and late, the hymns, and the translations. Bailey adopted the more nearly chronological order of the "Globe" edition. Annotation in Milford is sparse and is chiefly textual. Bailey's annotation is far more extensive. In the end, however, in spite of their divergences, the two volumes tend to supplement each other rather than to cancel each other out. Both are necessary to a thorough study of the poetry.

So much for the problems of the text. The critical problems are more extensive.

If there have been people at least as early as Lord Byron who have denied Cowper the right to be called a poet at all, there are still those today—as I suggested earlier—who consider him "first and foremost . . . an Evangelical preacher" or at best an essayist in verse somewhat in the manner of Charles

Lamb in prose. His verse, as we have also seen, has been accounted "only a little above mediocrity" and "second-rate of various degrees." On the other hand, most critical appraisals have taken the position that, whatever his relative merit may be among English poets as a group, he has an enduring appeal, the ingredients of which are worthy of examination.

It is true that among those who insist upon his considerable value both as a poet and as a letter writer a kind of *je ne sais quoi* has served as the ultimate explanation of his appeal, though any number of more specific qualities have been adduced. Among these are "the antiseptic grace of humane sincerity,"[413] "a certain childlike quality of innocence . . . associated with a mature and vivid perception of objects in their primary power to heal and inform the human spirit,"[304] a "simplicity which . . . saw beauty in common things,"[320] the transmutation of "good sense into true poetry"[392]—to list only a few. Great art, most sympathetic critics of the poet have admitted, is (in Arnold's phrase) that which sees life steadily and sees it whole. At the same time, they may contend, there is a perfectly defensible art that sees a segment of life steadily and makes an artistic whole out of what it sees. E. M. Forster[335] has commented on Cowper in this way:

> Of course, he was an invalid, and his attachment to local scenes can be discounted on that account. He had not enough vitality to seek new experiences, and never felt safe until habits had formed their cocoon round his sensitive mind. But inside the cocoon his life is genuine. He might dread the unknown, but he also loved what he knew; he felt steadily about familiar objects, and they have in his work something of the permanence they get in a sitting-room or in a kitchen garden.

The fact that he is a "little" poet, the general argument has run, does not mean that he cannot be a "good" poet. And there have certainly been implications—even though the point may not have been explicitly stated—that an appreciation of Cowper may actually be an acquired taste, an evidence of maturity and perhaps, specifically, a feeling for an essential and peculiar quality of English-ness in the poetry and the letters—as Birrell[309] and Forster,[335] among others, have suggested.

For the same reason that it has been difficult to isolate the exact qualities of Cowper's permanence, other aspects of his work—his literary indebtedness, for example—have not lent themselves as readily to the same sort of scholarly treatment as have the works of other poets.

Although we cannot accept the complete accuracy of Cowper's assertion that his descriptions were all from nature ("not one of them second-handed"), that his "delineations of the heart" were from his own experience ("not one of them borrowed from books"), and that he "imitated nobody," these contentions are at least true enough to make source- and influence-hunting in his poetry an unexciting game. The main influences have generally seemed so clear as to demand little elaboration; the minor ones, so negligible as to be unworthy of extended effort. Early influences of John Philips and Matthew Prior were admitted by the poet himself. Critics have not infrequently observed that Cowper is an "extension" of Thomson,[340] and there has been some attempt to indicate the influence of Young.[441] The influences of Horace[381] and Milton[430] have been observed as being "pervasive," but in most instances matters of assimilation rather than imitation. And if many extended studies of the poetry have observed the influence of Homer, certainly all of them have noted the influence of the Bible. A brief study has been made of the possible influence of Vaughan[436] on Cowper's attitude toward Nature, and a more lengthy effort has been made to explore the influence of the Methodist rhapsodist, James Hervey, in the same area.[432] The generally assumed influence of Charles Churchill has been challenged, though not entirely convincingly.[431] Rather than to point out the influence of Pope, it has perhaps been more cus-

tomary to contend simply that Cowper was everything that
Pope was not.

Though the problem of placing the poet in the literary context of his own century has by no means generated so heated an
argument as the problem of the relationship between his religion
and his poetic inspiration, it has given rise to a considerable
difference of opinion between a large group of literary critics
and historians who have wished to regard him as a precursor of
Romanticism and a smaller but quite persistent group who have
labeled him as a late neo-classicist.   In short, he has been
called everything from a "leader"[300] in the "poetic revival of
1760-1820" to "a defiant rearguard"[324] in the ranks of the neo-
classicists.   On the other hand, legitimate protests have been
made to the effect that picturing Cowper as anything so strong
as a leader or a fighter in any cause can find little corroboration
in his character[390] and that plausible evidence can be adduced
from his work pointing toward both Romanticism and neo-
classicism.

At one extreme is an amusingly vigorous but scarcely
judicious opinion expressed in 1913 by Edward Storer, who as
editor of a small book of selections from Cowper[141] wrote an
introduction in which he used his subject chiefly to belabor
what he considered to be "the decadent and lifeless romanticism" of the time—the period just before World War I. Cowper, Storer insists, was "an anti-Romantic, an Augustan though
domiciliary poet" who had been denied anything but "a
grudging and rather contemptuous appreciation" because of
"one hundred years of the domination of a romantic criterion
for art."   Unfortunately, his final judgment of the poet is
tinged with anti-climax: "though he is not a great classicist, he
is nothing at all of a romantic."   More recently Donald Davie
has argued for regarding Cowper as a neo-classicist with ampler
evidence than Storer produced—and with less special plead-
ing.[324]

Saintsbury, on the other hand, resolved the dilemma by

finding in Cowper's work "the oddest mixture of the old and the new."[389] Yet, whereas he saw the poet as a sort of literary Janus facing both ways, he felt that Cowper ultimately inclined toward the old rather than toward the new. Perhaps too uncertain of their ground to call him simply "a poet *sui generis*" (as the critic in the *Monthly Review* did in 1782), an increasing number of critics have been inclined to call him "a transitional poet" and to consider that in so doing the job of classification has been done as well as it can be.

The first major biographers of Cowper—Hayley and Southey—were themselves practicing poets. And so have been two contemporary ones—Fausset and Thomas. Thus a good deal of perceptive critical comment has been made along the way. Even biographers like Smith, Elwin, and Quinlan, not themselves poets, have spent much of their time as "critical biographers."

The close union of biography and criticism has been understandably responsible for making a major critical problem of the relationship of religion to the poet's inspiration and achievement. Fausset's general position of denying anything good to Evangelicalism naturally caused him to give little credit to religion as a constructive force in Cowper's literary production. His poetry, Fausset argued, was simply a kind of "self-defense," and the tragedy of his life was that "he could not transform poetry as a means of self-defense into a vehicle of creative imagination."

This kind of opinion, if not always so forcefully expressed, has not been entirely confined to Fausset. In fact, Louise Lanham, who takes the opposite view, has been willing to assume that literary study has regularly tended to regard Evangelicalism as a deleterious influence on the poet's art.[359] (She was not, of course, unaware that a staunch group—including at least Smith, Elwin, Birrell, Hannay, and the anonymous reviewer of Fausset's "Everyman" edition of the *Poems* in the Times *Literary Supplement*[378]—had argued otherwise.)

Most of Cowper's poetry, Miss Lanham asserts, is organical-
ly related to his religious experience. She establishes a direct
connection between his Evangelical stimulus in the controversy
over Martin Madan's *Thelyphthora* and his embarking on his
first major poetic effort (a contention corroborated in another
independent study[806]); and she finds a definite nexus between
the anti-slavery sentiments of the Evangelical group and Cowper's own. In fact, she argues that most of the didactic poems
or satires (except in those elements consciously introduced to
lighten them) were "dictated" by his religion. Countering the
well-established tendency to overrate the "worldly" influence
of Lady Austen in *The Task*, Miss Lanham contends not only
that there is nothing in the poem to conflict with Cowper's
Evangelicalism but also that his love of nature and his general
humanitarianism are integrally related to his faith. The
poésie domestique, too, she sees as an aspect of his "essential
Puritanism."

Norman Nicholson's critical monograph also examines in
detail the relationship to the Evangelical revival, showing
how Cowper was able to join "a great movement of popular
thought" and to participate in "the fears and excitements of
people from many levels of society" and how he was able to
forget in this experience "much of his self-consciousness and
much of his sense of isolation."[373] "Without the Revival,"
Nicholson says in summary, "he would never have become a
poet, for it gave him a deep emotional experience, a prolonged
fervour which for many months lifted him like a love affair
above the compromises and consequences of everyday life."
Nicholson also examines the relationship between the Revival
and the Romantic Movement, particularly in the way in which
Cowper's poetry reflected the return to nature and the country-
side and the distrust of reason.

There is nothing new, of course, in Nicholson's contention
that though Cowper's life had much sadness in it "his poetry
was largely the poetry of pleasure" or that though he was at

times mad "his poetry is essentially the poetry of the sane"; nor is there anything original in the assertion that Cowper was "the poet of the ordinary, everyday country" who became "the spokesman for the conscience of the middle classes." But as a practicing poet himself, the critic is able to make a sensitive analysis of the poetic elements in the hymns, an acute exposition of the use of "shifting focus" in the descriptive poetry, and a fresh appraisal of the achievement of the Homeric translations.

Comparable with the consideration of Cowper's religious experience as a deterrent or a stimulus to his creative effort—and, of course, closely related to it—is the matter of the effect of the poet's suffering on his art. Neilson C. Hannay, for example, has suggested that suffering acted as a "valuable restraining influence" ultimately exerting a far-reaching effect on Cowper's style and message.[346] For many years, Hannay remarks, the poet's perceptions were "somewhat cloyed by his classical heritage and his imitative instinct." Not only did suffering act as a catharsis to create in Cowper the best qualities of his maturity, but it also enabled the poet to focus his native indolence and to turn it into significant creative activity under the impetus of pain.

In an attempt to explain the continuing appeal of Cowper to readers of the mid-twentieth century, Kenneth MacLean takes a different tack.[367] Echoing Fausset's earlier assertion that Cowper's poetry was written "on the edge of an abyss,"[120] MacLean argues that the poetry and the letters maintain their appeal because they are "a record of a terror." Not content with merely regarding pain or terror as the informing force in the poetry, the critic goes considerably further afield. "Neurosis and not the romantic movement," he asserts sweepingly, "was responsible for everything that [Cowper] was as a writer." This, it will be quite clear, is the most comprehensive psychoneurological thesis that has yet been developed.

Since Cowper has not been regarded widely as a poet of

ideas, his place in the history of eighteenth-century thought has not been given a great deal of consideration. Some attention has been paid, however, to his similarities to Rousseau and to his attitude both toward the natural man and toward nature. And his criticism of eighteenth-century educational theory and practice, particularly in the public schools, has been taken seriously.[316] Recently a thoroughgoing examination has been made of his references to science for the purpose of establishing in detail his relationship to the anti-rationalism of the end of the century.[358]

His humanitarianism has also been studied at length in *William Cowper: Humanitarian*, not only as a part of the Revival, but also as a part of the literary and social traditions of the century.[349] Though Cowper has often been considered to be isolated and provincial, the study argues, the things that he commented upon when he looked out from his "loophole of retreat" were some of the most important humanitarian, social, and political concerns of the century: the problems of philanthropy, the abolition of slavery, the plight of India, the need for Poor Law and prison reforms, the moral inadequacies of British education. On these matters, the study further demonstrates, the poet definitely had ideas which he was able to express with sanity, strength, and courage. The whole is intended to serve as a corrective to any notion that Cowper was merely a mild and amiable valetudinarian.

Studies relating to particular works of the poet, while in some instances repeating the general critical and biographical arguments, have at times contributed significant new material.

The great popularity of the *Olney Hymns* has made a discussion of them a necessity in any standard treatment of English hymnology. Their doctrinal content has naturally been studied in relation to their total religious milieu. In recent years their religious and autobiographical qualities have been the subject of some debate. H. N. Fairchild, for example, insists that even though the hymns are often written in the first person, "they are seldom very specifically subjective"[334]; and Wendell M. Keck, in the most elaborate theological study of the hymns to date, concludes that "the personal tone of these testimonials" should be taken "as conventional expression, not as Cowperian autobiography."[510]   Canon Benham's older opinion ("All Cowper's hymns throw light upon his mental state at that time, and there are several allusions to the circumstances of his life")[106] has been supported with some conviction and documentation by Gillman,[506] Thomas,[280] Nicholson,[373] and Hartley.[508]   The last named suggests that a reading of the hymns in the order in which they are printed in the published volume (in spite of the fact that this is not the chronological order of their composition) will reveal the impression of "an intensely personal struggle for a faith."   Nicholson observes that though Cowper derives more directly from the sweeping vistas, the boldness, and the simplicity of Watt, he is often close to the vividly personal tone of Wesley, and that he, in fact, bridges "the gap between the devotional poem (the personal expression of a personal feeling) and the hymn."

Gillman, interestingly enough, thinks that the subjective quality is one of the reasons that many of the hymns are unfit for congregational singing; whereas Nicholson contends that the reason for Cowper's "comparative failure" as a hymn writer was that he himself was not really a "hymn *singer.*"

Cowper's hymns have many times been warmly admired or perhaps even warmly disliked by people who have no notion about their authorship; thus they have had a vivid existence apart from the biography of the poet or from his major work. "John Gilpin" is another work that has had a lively history and an audience of its own.   In the main, printed comments on the poem have been made by amateurs and antiquarians rather than by scholars, and the many attempts to identify the hero as an actual person[607] and to mark out the exact route of the famous ride[605] have provided more entertainment than enlightenment.   The notable exception is a double article by Max

Förster[606] providing a detailed and scholarly treatment of the
complicated story of the text, the dissemination of the ballad,
the continuations, and the translations.

Any need for critical comment on the poem has seemed
gratuitous, for it has provided pure delight to young and old
for almost two centuries, and it has proved a ready inspiration
to illustrators and book designers. A rare dissenting voice
like that of Norman Nicholson, therefore, demands quoting—
almost as a curiosity:

> I can raise scarcely a grin at the antics of the mis-
> erable linen-draper, and I am surprised that Cowper
> could laugh at the misfortunes of a rider on a frantic,
> runaway horse without, apparently, giving one thought
> to the horse. It seems to me, indeed, that Cowper is
> rarely funny when he is *trying* to be funny.[373]

"John Gilpin" was a *jeu d'esprit* at the beginning of Cowper's late entrance into the field of published poets. Its wild-
fire success was not only surprising but it was even in a measure
embarrassing. After the somewhat less sensational though far
more solid success of *The Task*, there came the long devotion to
the translation of Homer—a project that fell short of unquali-
fied approval in the poet's own day and has continued to do so
since. In the preface to his edition of the *Poetical Works* in
1905, Humphrey Milford announced with somber finality: "the
translation of Homer is dead." Five years later, nevertheless,
J. M. Dent elected to bring out Cowper's translation of the
Odyssey in the Everyman Series.[125]

Plainly, the Homeric translations have had little scholarly
attention in the twentieth century, critics generally agreeing
with Matthew Arnold's comment on their lack of "rapidity" if
not entirely with Milford's virtual epitaph. Cowper knew
Homer, Harold Child observed, "but his head was full of
Milton. Homer is grand and lively, Cowper's *Homer* is grand
and dull."[320] And Fausset remarks: "Homer was for Cowper

something of a 'venerable old gentleman.' "[227] Although his appreciation of the original simplicity was enough to allow him to see the meretriciousness of Pope, the critic continues, Cowper himself "lacked the natural energy which dictated the simplicity." From another point of view Gilbert Thomas explains the failure of the translations by observing that "Cowper . . . was unable to sympathize or square his conscience with the passions of a primitive world."[280]

Norman Nicholson, after a fresh and sensitive reading of the *Homer*, declares himself in favor.[373] Though he accepts the general opinion about excessive Miltonisms in the poems, he calls them "competent, easy, and, on the whole, interesting." Sometimes, he allows, they even "smoulder into poetry." Cowper, it is true, was no match for Pope in epigrammatic brilliance; but at least in the *Odyssey* he excelled in straightforward narrative, where his telling realism had a definite advantage over Pope's artificial glitter.[811]

Apart from the Homeric poems, there were also Cowper's translations from Italian and Latin, most of which—and especially those from Milton[135]—have continued to be held in high esteem and to be frequently reprinted. Because of their obvious relationship to the poet's religious involvement, more attention has been paid in recent years to Cowper's translations from the French of Madame Guyon.

Actually, one of the earliest of the biographies (the little *Memoirs* issued from the London bookshop of T. Williams in 1803) pointed out the "superiority" of Cowper's translations to the original French, demonstrating how the translator eliminated religious eroticism and "levity" in the original:

> Mme. Guyon seldom speaks of Christ by any other title than that of her *husband* or *love* . . . her expressions are sometimes tinctured with childishness and levity. These her translator has corrected with the usual delicacy of his taste.[807]

The anonymous biographer is also careful to point out the essential differences between the Quietism of the French poet and the Evangelicalism of the English one.

A far more elaborate study of the translations was made in 1939 by Dorothy L. Gilbert and Russell Pope.[804] Though the conclusions are the same, this study shows in detail the ways in which Cowper deleted and revised to temper the religious fanaticism of the original, occasionally injecting typical Evangelical phrases.

Since the letters occupy a place of first importance not only in an interpretation of Cowper's life (as one would naturally expect) but also in an understanding of the poetry, the rather late consideration of them and their problems in this discussion can best be explained by pointing out the fact that their importance has, in a sense, been assumed throughout.

"William Cowper," Thomas Wright began the preface to his edition of the *Correspondence*, "is universally acknowledged to be the greatest of letter writers."[151] This sweeping claim, though supported by Saintsbury and others, might be disputed. Nevertheless, it is true that regardless of the gradations of opinion concerning Cowper as a poet, his reputation as a letter writer has been uniformly high. Professor Chauncey B. Tinker has remarked that the letters of the eighteenth century achieve a "smiling intimacy," a new quality of epistolary style.[944] Cowper's letters, almost every critic old or new has admitted, are among the most charming of the century because they have a rare intimacy, being totally without self-conscious art or pretense. Pope, as it is well known, surreptitiously brought out an edition of his own letters, Sterne kept a letter book to preserve his private correspondence for whatever later use he might want to make of it, and Walpole apparently selected his correspondents with a view to making his letters of the broadest possible use to posterity. Unlike any of these, Cowper recorded for his friends the simple daily life of a provincial village with an elegance and a deliberateness that were the outgrowth both of his leisure and his culture, yet with a spontaneity as fresh as the English atmosphere after a shower of rain. "He never forgot," Mark Van Doren has observed, "that his friends wanted to hear of him, not from him. So it was of himself he talked—where he had walked that morning, what he was wearing, and how he felt and thought."[145]

Although a great deal has been written about the letters in the period covered by this survey, no impressively new critical opinions have been advanced. E. V. Lucas sees Cowper as "the father of whimsicality" (of which Lamb was the chief popularizer) and "the first to handle the new prose,"[921] whereas W. H. Irving regards Cowper, along with Walpole, as "almost the last exponents" of "atticism" or effortless limpidity and simple elegance in letter writing.[917] There is no disparity between the two positions. Robert Lynd, like a number of others, has been inclined to feel that Cowper's final reputation rests on his letters rather than on the less satisfactory quality of his poetry.[922] Lytton Strachey emerges as one of the rare detractors. Although Cowper mastered the art of saying nothing well, Strachey contended, his letters are "stricken with sterility . . . dried up" and lacking "the juices of life."[941]

The most pitiable and the most frustrating fact about the letters is that now over a century and a half after Cowper's death there is still no reasonably complete and accurate edition of them.

The first attempt to print the letters as a part of Hayley's *Life* was most unfortunate in that Hayley, working under the strict limitations imposed by Lady Hesketh, mutilated and suppressed the letters in a way that can only give a chill of horror to any modern editor. Lady Hesketh's wish, as she expressed it to John Johnson, was that nothing should be brought forward that should cause her distinguished cousin "to be considered as a Visionary! an Enthusiast! or a *Calvinist*," since she was "*very sure* he was neither in reality." Thus Hayley—deleting single words, phrases, sentences, paragraphs, making miscellaneous substitutions, and even suppressing whole letters—omitted references to the most personal of his subject's religious beliefs. But he did not stop with these. Out, too, went most of Cowper's frankest revelations of himself (particularly his moments of despair), references to his family and friends (lest people still living should object), and even Cowper's humorous comment on the world around him. Indeed, Hayley wrote to Lady Hesketh in a sentence that sums up much of the tragedy of his editorial license, "I suppressed perhaps *even more*, than I printed."

John Johnson's edition of the *Private Correspondence* printed letters not included in Hayley with a double purpose—not so ironical or conflicting as it may seem on the surface—of demonstrating Cowper's religious notions and, at the same time, of revealing his more playful moods, which Hayley had deemed it desirable to conceal from the public.

Grimshawe's edition was, in Kenneth Povey's phrase, a "clumsy rehandling of Hayley's [edition] inspired by a ludicrous zeal for the interests of religion and morality,"[933] plus a reprinting of the letters from the *Private Correspondence*, to which Grimshawe had access but Southey did not. Grimshawe's fault was general incompetence. Southey's failings, on the other hand, were rather a matter of circumstance. Because Southey could see only a limited number of the original letters, he was forced to perpetuate many of Hayley's mutilations—a large portion of which have never been corrected.

In 1904 Thomas Wright brought out what he modestly called a "practically complete" edition, containing 1041 letters.[151] Approximately three-fourths of these were wholly from Southey and fewer than 250 were unpublished or partly published. Although Wright had seen about four hundred original letters which he had compared with Southey's text, he unfortunately failed to indicate which letters he had collated and which he had not. Thus in a given letter one has no assurance of reliability beyond that of Southey's text.

Immediately after the publication of Wright's edition, J. E. B. Mayor in a series of communications to *Notes and Queries* indicated a considerable number of additions and corrections;[925] and more recently Kenneth Povey, himself an enthusiastic student of the letters, has convincingly argued the unreliability of all existing texts, demonstrating graphically the ways in which Hayley's mutilations were made and perpetuated.[933]

Since 1904 a number of new letters have been discovered; and both these and the correct versions of inaccurately printed letters have appeared in various journals. Moreover, Bailey, in his edition of the *Poems* in 1905, printed 35 letters to Joseph Hill and to John and Catharine Johnson;[104] in 1925 Wright brought out a small volume of the *Unpublished and Uncollected Letters of Cowper*;[152] and in 1959 in an appendix to his study of the young Cowper, Ryskamp printed a small group of uncollected letters written between 1750 and 1767.[937]

Selections of letters have largely reprinted Southey's text, though Mark Van Doren[145] used Wright's.

For over thirty years Neilson C. Hannay has been engaged in a definitive edition of the letters—tirelessly tracking down the originals, collating them, and acquiring as many as possible for his own private collection. He now has what is beyond question the most complete collection of original letters and accurate copies of existing letters. Until his edition appears, Cowperian scholarship in several areas must mark time.

A recent exchange of views among Maurice Quinlan, Norma Hodgson Russell,[11] and Charles Ryskamp[16] regarding two rival editions of Cowper's autobiography highlights the general bibliographical neglect of the poet. Although rare Cowper items have at times appeared in sales catalogues and although some few of them have demanded prices indicative of considerable collector's interest, until now there has been no reliable comprehensive guide to Cowperian bibliography beyond the list in the *British Museum Catalogue of Printed Books*.[3] Sporadic interest in the bibliography has produced no appreciable results. Fortunately, the genuine need for careful bibliographical study will be met for the most significant period of publication by Mrs. Russell's forthcoming double volume in the Oxford Bibliographical Society series to be published in 1960. Ranging from Cowper's earliest work to Southey's final volume in the complete works in 1837, it is divided into twelve roughly chronological sections as follows: i., the early years in the Temple; ii., the *Olney Hymns* and other hymns by Cowper, with close attention to the first publication of hymns in periodicals; iii., *Anti-Thelyphthora*; iv., poems, including collected editions before 1837 and publication of single poems in periodicals, miscellanies, *et cetera*, and in chapbook form plus continuations and imitations; v., reviews in the *Analytical Review*; vi., translations (other than those included in i); vii., posthumous prose works (the *Memoir* and letters); viii., works edited or revised by Cowper; ix., collected editions; x., biographies of Cowper (including important notices in periodicals); xi., Cowperiana: topographical volumes, works dedicated to Cowper, poetical tributes, answers to Cowper, selections from Cowper, songbooks, *et cetera*; xii., iconography (the original portraits and engravings from them, a lost portrait, spurious or doubtful portraits).

Mrs. Russell's work may be expected to be the most elaborate piece of Cowperian bibliographical scholarship yet undertaken. The fact that it has been projected is indicative of the kind of painstaking and objective attention the poet is now getting.

Other works in progress include a definitive biography and several studies of the poetry. One may hope ultimately for Cowper the same kind of careful editorial treatment that Pope, Johnson, Boswell, Walpole and others are receiving from contemporary scholars. Clearly the field is still open; and, as the number of studies in the last two decades alone would indicate, there is quite enough momentum and enthusiasm to keep conspicuously alive a well-deserved interest in Cowper both as poet and letter writer.

IV

THE ASPECT OF PERMANENCE: A
RECAPITULATION

One should not have to argue further that for a complete view of English literature Cowper will still have to be read because, in spite of his apparent isolation, he reflects not only important aspects of eighteenth-century religious, political, and ethical thought but also aspects of the essential British character, or because he mirrors important changes that were taking place in English taste. It should also be clear that these reasons do not exhaust the possibilities. One ought, of course, to be able always to discover elements of appeal in a poet's work apart from its relationship to a particular time or place. Ample evidence has been given that these elements have been adduced in reasonable number, though not all the arguments for them have avoided the so-called fallacy of assuming the man and his poetry to be inseparable.

The assumption that readers will universally react to the pain or the terror that lies behind the calm exterior of most of the verse and the letters has been frequently relied upon as the most likely basis of permanent interest. Certainly, the terror of damnation that hung over the poet for a large part of his life, harrowing him in his dreams, driving him to suicide attempts, and sinking him into periods of imbecilic melancholia has long contributed to the sympathetic reading that many have given to his verse. But an overemphasis on the pathetic aspects of his literary production has for too long tended to obscure other

qualities that offer equally legitimate arguments for permanence.

Even admitting terror to be the informing force behind
every line of Cowper's verse or prose, it could be sensed in many
instances only by those who are well acquainted with the facts
of the poet's life. In the often quoted Sapphics, ending

> *I*, fed with judgment, in a fleshly tomb, am
>   Buried above ground,

the terror, everywhere apparent, is case history rather than
poetry. The terror in short lyrics like "The Shrubbery" and
"The Castaway" happens to produce poetry before it produces
case history. But one cannot read the whole of Cowper's
poetry merely as if it were the record of a neurosis. Certainly,
much of the verse is capable of being read otherwise. And no
matter how much an acquaintance with the poet's suffering
may enhance an appreciation of the poetry, the appeal of the
verse must rest finally on something beyond a sensitivity to the
tragic circumstances out of which it arose.

In spite of the fact that I may not entirely avoid the common fallacy in so doing, I suggest that the most apposite explanation of the continuing appeal of Cowper lies in the con-
sequence of his pervading conviction of singularity, a belief in
uniqueness that can shine through a line of poetry or prose with
the immediate effect of delight or terror—delight most often
and terror only rarely.

It cannot be denied that Cowper's most explicit assertion of
this singularity arose as a concomitant of the terror of which
the poet's critics and biographers have been keenly conscious.
The *locus classicus* is a letter written in 1763 only a short time
before Cowper's first really serious breakdown. "I am of a very
singular temper," he wrote to his cousin Harriet Cowper (later
Lady Hesketh), "and very unlike all the men that I have ever
conversed with." Nineteen years later he wrote to his friend,
the Reverend William Bull: ". . . there is no encouragement in

the Scripture so comprehensive as to include *my* case [the italics are mine], nor any consolation so effective as to reach it." The neurosis is here for all to see.

Interestingly enough, at least two other geniuses of the eighteenth century, neither one free of neuroses, had convictions of singularity.   Young Boswell's is expressed with characteristic brashness in a letter to Rousseau in December, 1764: "Open your door, then, Sir, to a man who dares to tell you that he deserves to enter it.   Place your confidence in a stranger who is different."   Much closer to Cowper's statement is a famous one of Rousseau himself, whose malady was nearer Cowper's and who had difficulty in escaping his more worldly terrors similar to that which Cowper had in hiding from his fear of hell-fire.   "I am made unlike any one I have ever met," Rousseau began the *Confessions*; "I will even venture to say that I am like no one in the whole world."

This feeling of uniqueness seems to have imbued the climate of the age.   Whether it arose out of a reaction to the classic emphasis on the similarities of men or to the philosophic idea that men were mere links in a chain stretching down from God to nature, or whether it could be attributed to individual neuroses, it is difficult to say.   At any rate, from whatever basis and with whatever different effect, Rousseau, Boswell, and Cowper shared a fundamental belief in singularity; and each was able to translate that belief with amazing directness and ingenuousness (and here is the real secret) into enduring literature.

On something less than the pathological side, easily apparent evidences of Cowper's feeling of uniqueness lie in his mild but stubborn independence of conventional values.   For example, on September 2, 1762, we find the young Templar writing to a friend:

> . . . a covetous dog who will work by candlelight in a
> morning, to get what he does not want, shall be praised

for his thriftiness, while a gentleman shall be abused for submitting to his wants, rather than work like an ass to relieve them. . . . All this is nonsense, and nothing better. . . . Upon the whole, my dear Rowley, there is a degree of poverty that has no disgrace belonging to it; that degree of it, I mean, in which a man enjoys clean linen and good company; and if I never sink below this degree of it, I care not if I never rise above it.

This is not exactly like saying with Thoreau in the next century:

If a man walk in the woods for love of them half of each day, he is in danger of being regarded as a loafer; but if he spends his whole day as a speculator, shearing off those woods and making earth bald before her time, he is esteemed an industrious and enterprising citizen.

But as a gentleman and a lover of nature, Cowper could have subscribed as unreservedly to Thoreau's statement as Thoreau could have subscribed to his. And, slight though the evidence may be, it is symbolic of a significant character trait.

It is, of course, possible to regard Cowper simply as the literary amateur *par excellence*. Certainly he never wrote for material gain; moreover, his independence of literary fashions makes his removal from Grub Street seem far more remote than his removal from other aspects of the world from which he had "retired." Writing for him was for a long time a combination of gentlemanly amusement and occupational therapy. Even as a young man he confessed that he wrote—

> to divert a fierce banditti
> (Sworn foes to ev'ry thing that's witty),
> That, with a black infernal train,
> Make cruel inroads in my brain.

In later life he wrote more explicitly to Lady Hesketh, referring to his attack of melancholia in 1773:

As soon as I became capable of action, I commenced carpenter, made cupboards, boxes, stools. . . . To this employment succeeded that of gardening, which I intermingled with that of drawing, but finding that the latter injured my eyes, I renounced it, and commenced poet.

And to William Unwin he wrote:

I have no more right to the name of a poet than a maker of mouse-traps has to that of an engineer; but my little exploits in this way have at times amused me so much, that I have often wished myself a good one. Such a talent in verse as mine is like a child's rattle,—very entertaining to the trifler that uses it, and very disagreeable to all beside. But it has served to rid me of some melancholy moments, for I only take it up as a gentleman performer does his fiddle.

But the whole story is not here. Charming amateur that Cowper was, he wanted something better. Once having embarked as a published poet, he aspired to make the best possible "mouse-trap"—not so much that the world would beat a path to his door but that he might break out of his psychic prison-house and that his tortured life might have some palpable justification. The other side of the coin is revealed in a letter to Lady Hesketh of May 15, 1786:

. . . till lately, I stole through life without undertaking any thing, yet always wishing to distinguish myself. At last I ventured, ventured, too, in the only path that at so late a period was yet open to me; and am determined, if God have not determined otherwise, to work my way through the obscurity, that has been so long my portion, into notice.

When notice was accorded him, he could exclaim, "It is a noble thing to be a poet, it makes the world so lively." This signifi-

cant desire for self-assertion and for recognition—apparent
even when on occasions he denied it—has too often gone unnoticed. It is a positive aspect of Cowper's conviction of
singularity without which his achievement would not have
been possible. The conviction of uniqueness and the desire to
assert this uniqueness may thus be regarded as twin aspects of
Cowper's creative effort.

The substance of what Cowper wished to achieve and what
he thought he had achieved is summed up in a well-known letter
that he wrote in 1784 to William Unwin concerning a draft of
The Task:

> My descriptions are all from nature: not one of them
> second-handed. My delineations of the heart are from
> my own experience: not one of them borrowed from
> books or in the least degree conjectural. In my numbers
> . . . I have imitated nobody, though sometimes perhaps
> there may be an apparent resemblance; because at the
> same time I would not imitate, I have not affectedly
> differed.

This is a quiet but eloquent manifesto—no preface to *Lyrical
Ballads*, it is true, but a climactic expression of an independence
and an individuality that, though often obscured by his malady,
did not die within him until he sank into his final insanity.

In a sense, his whole poetic development—unusual and
irregular though it was—led up to the statement; for manifestations of his particular spirit somehow break through most
of the inhibitions under which he wrote. With such an idea in
mind an examination of the broad lines of his development may
be worthwhile.

Though he emerged very late as a popular poet, he had
written poetry most of his life. Flashes of his youthful verse—
some of them terrible—reveal presentiments of his peculiar fate
and—like his letters—assertions of singularity. But most of
them, it is true, rather picture for us a shy, witty, and reasona-

bly talented young man who wrote quasi-erotic poetry aspiring to the "smoothness" of Waller, together with miscellaneous verse showing affinity for "Mat Prior's easy jingle."

Cowper was over forty when his first considerable group of poems appeared in print in *The Olney Hymns*. This was the result of a collaboration that was fortunate in producing some fine hymns and unfortunate in that it finally failed in the healing of Cowper's distressed mind for which it was intended. Here was a project in which the assignments were determined by Cowper's Evangelical friend, the Reverend John Newton, and in which verse patterns and imagery were dictated by the milieu as well as the medium. Yet even under such restrictions Cowper gave his hymns a sense of personal poignance, employing homely imagery with vivid effect and investing stock figures with freshness. "Oh! for a Closer Walk with God," "God Moves in a Mysterious Way," and "There Is a Fountain Fill'd with Blood" are all models of conformity to which Cowper added varying measures of originality and poetic inspiration. But only a hymn writer bold enough to assert total independence of the clichés of the craft could produce such an amusingly realistic and unhymnlike stanza as the following:

> What trifles tease me now!
> They swarm like summer flies,
> They cleave to ev'ry thing I do,
> And swim before my eyes.

The hymns were a kind of controlled exercise. Some of the same control remained for the poems of the 1782 volume—but with a difference. Many of Cowper's biographers still attribute his first major effort to Mrs. Unwin's prodding. This was not strictly true. Actually, Cowper began writing satires with a little mock-heroic poem called *Anti-Thelyphthora*. As it turned out, this minor foray into the ridiculous Madan controversy over the biblical justification for polygamy was not entirely a happy one; but the impetus that Cowper developed in his satirical effort carried over into *The Progress of Error* and other poems eventually included in the 1782 volume. Though all were composed under the general aegis of Newton, the real initiative was Cowper's own. The impulse to self-expression thus induced developed into a genuine poetic *furor*.

Whereas earlier reviews of the 1782 volume were only luke-warm, the *Monthly Review* boldly acclaimed Cowper "a poet *sui generis*," whose "notes are peculiar to himself" and "who classes not with any species of bards that have preceded him." This recognition of singularity was understandably pleasing to Cowper. To readers of today the validity of such a judgment may not be at all clear. First, Cowper seems to make no revolt from current satirical practice: the general tradition followed is Horatian, the verse form is the heroic couplet, and at times the poetry echoes Dryden and Pope, or the poet's old school friend, Charles Churchill. Second, if the unique contribution of the volume—as the *Monthly Review* has it—is the unusual blend of the "serious and devotional" with the "dryly humorous and the sarcastic," this quality may be obscured simply because in some of the poetry Cowper sounds more like an Evangelical preacher than like a satirist or a poet of any sort.

At his worst in the poems, he declaims like any revivalist against card-playing, dancing, and drinking. He attacks the Deists, the Catholics, the atheists, the scientists, the rationalists. He strikes out at corruption in the clergy. He preaches a sermon on grace against works. He turns Jeremiah and prophesies national ruin because of national iniquity. Too often, in short, we may feel that he is writing not what his inclination would lead him to write so much as what John Newton, Mrs. Unwin, and other Evangelical friends *expected* him to write. This inhibition—quite apart from the argument that his religion frequently gave him both consolation and inspiration—may well account for much of the homiletic dullness, as well as for occasional touches of bigotry in the poems.

Yet even in pieces like *The Progress of Error, Truth, Expostu-*

lation, Hope, and *Charity* there are flashes of the poet's essential
genius as, for example, when he pays his respects to the
eighteenth-century idea that travel is broadening:

> How much a dunce that has been sent to roam
> Excels a dunce that has been kept at home—

or when he speaks warmly and courageously against social
injustices, including slavery:

> Nature imprints upon whate'er we see
> That has a heart and life in it.—Be free!
> . . . .
> . . . souls have no discriminating hue,
> Alike important in their Maker's view.

The other long poems in the volume have more claim to
freshness and individuality. *Table Talk,* designed to introduce
the volume and to "decoy" readers into it, is less heavily
didactic. In it we hear the "recluse of Olney" discuss, often
with independence and sound reasoning, a wide variety of
things from British military conduct in the American war to the
essential mission of poetry. We detect an authentic voice
speaking against

> . . . admirals, extoll'd for standing still,
> Or doing nothing with a deal of skill;
> Gen'rals who will not conquer when they may,
> Firm friends to peace, to pleasure, and good pay,

or sense a beginning of revolt in the assertion that Pope, though
he "gave virtue and morality a grace . . . Made poetry a mere
mechanic art."

Conversation, based—if somewhat remotely—on a youthful
essay written for the *Connoisseur* is still lighter in tone. By this
time Lady Austen had come to Olney and her mild liberation of
Cowper from his more somber Evangelical connections was
beginning to be felt. But the Evangelical coloring is still

present, particularly in the castigation of bawdy and blasphemous talk and the strong disapproval of tobacco—"pernicious weed." Cowper makes a more universal approach in satirizing those bores who tell interminable stories or talk about their ancestry or their health:

Some men employ their health, an ugly trick,
In making known how oft they have been sick.

 .   .   .   .

They thought they must have died they were so bad—
Their peevish hearers almost wish they had.

Without making a complete turn from the other poems, *Retirement* definitely points the way to *The Task* and to Cowper's most genuine contribution to English poetry. The poem belongs—it is clear—to an overworked tradition stemming from the pastoral, from Horace, from Cowley's essay "Of Myself," and from Pomfret's popular poem, "The Choice." The "retirement" in such poetry was usually an amiable and easily transparent affectation in which poets rejoiced in the country because it provided escape from the boredom of the city. Thus life in the country was praised chiefly because it was not life in the city. The phenomenon is a curious one. With the rise of *bourgeois* culture in the century, the "citizen" aspired to urbanity to escape the danger of being considered rustic or "gothic." At the same time, perhaps with the subconscious recognition that aristocracy is based on the land, he arrives at a limited rejection of urbanity in order to achieve an added elegance not to be acquired in the city! Thus we have the spectacle of the "cit" in his "country box," ridiculous because his artificial and *bourgeois* urbanity is so ill-fitting in a setting demanding natural and aristocratic rusticity. As Cowper puts it:

Tight boxes, neatly sash'd, and in a blaze
With all a July sun's collected rays,

> Delight a citizen, who, gasping there,
> Breathes clouds of dust, and calls it country air.

And he sums up the attitude of the typical *bourgeois* as follows:

> He likes the country, but in truth must own,
> Most likes it, when he studies it in town.

Cowper's assertion of his own singularity of attitude is at the heart of the poem. He has rejected the city, it is quite clear, but for reasons of his own. And he praises the country sincerely for the delights that the country offered and that he genuinely enjoyed. Quiet and peace had come to him—though not permanently—amid country scenes, and nature had offered him consoling joys. It is this conviction that he is able to transmit with genuine feeling.

"God made the country, and man made the town," Cowper was to say in *The Task*—the whole of which, he remarked to William Unwin, had "one tendency; to discountenance the modern enthusiasm after a London life, and to recommend rural ease and leisure, as friendly to the cause of piety and virtue."

But before he launched into this second major undertaking, he was destined to take a wonderfully uninhibited ride with a certain linen-draper named John Gilpin. The result was as unique in Cowper's work as it was in eighteenth-century literature in general.

Lady Austen had first told Cowper the story of John Gilpin's escapade. And, as everyone now knows, she also suggested the sofa as a subject. But contrary to many accounts of her, she was a proper Evangelical lady, not a brilliant, worldly butterfly. Moreover, in the composition of *The Task*, John Newton and, now more particularly, Mrs. Unwin had still to be reckoned with. So the new poem does not entirely escape the heavy hand of Evangelical sermonizing.

"Neither Cowper's piety nor his patriotism interests us today," Sir Herbert Grierson has remarked. Perhaps so. But if we have, indeed, made a drastic change from the widespread nineteenth-century attitude toward Cowper, it is not because we are incapable of being moved by religious poetry. It is rather because we seem better able to divine that much of Cowper's sermonizing does not arise from his essential self. We accept his conviction of damnation, at least as a kind of reality. But somehow to us the damned are not really convincing when they wield the scourge. They speak in their true voice only when out of their own personal suffering arises a feeling of kinship with all suffering mankind, a love and a sympathy for all sentient beings. This is why Cowper's religious satire often sounds hollow or pretentious. It is also why his treatment of humble life, of animals, and of the small things of nature best seen in *The Task* achieves a quiet eloquence rarely matched in English poetry.

The plan of *The Task* exquisitely reveals the peculiar quality of the poet. It is a minor masterpiece in the art of digression. But digression here is not the art of wandering from the subject to conceal want of matter, as Swift accounted it. Nor is it the kind of digression that makes *Tristram Shandy* the most wonderfully erratic of English novels. "Great wits jump," wrote Sterne. And they jump, as he plainly advertises, to the tune of Locke's theory of the association of ideas. In *Tristram Shandy*, Charles Whibley once suggested, attention is like a monkey swinging from limb to limb in the forest of the mind. The forest—the "contiguity of shade"—is in *The Task*, but hardly the monkey. Cowper's own explanation is simple enough: "the reflections are naturally suggested by the preceding paragraph." This is plainly the flow of easy conversation, with a natural passage from subject to subject sometimes so artless that one is hardly conscious of a change.

No less individual than the structure, and more of a break with the neo-classical tradition, is the blank verse. In this no one would maintain that Cowper was a trail-blazer. Thomson had used blank verse in the same sort of poetry and, like Cowper, his great model was John Milton. But Cowper imitated neither. If Thomson wrote much good blank verse, Cowper at his best could do better. Avoiding Thomson's frequent end-stopped lines that give the impression of unrhymed couplets, Cowper achieves greater flexibility and length of phrasing. Although he misses the vigor and sweep of Thomson, he has more ease and variety. And if he does not have the "organ" quality that he admired in Milton, he does develop a well-tuned stringed instrument that is both effective and distinctive.

Interestingly enough, Cowper becomes less plainly a neo-classical poet when he abandons the couplet, but he also re-veals how close to the main stream of classicism he is. The assertion of his own uniqueness and independence is clearly evidenced in his admiration for the "naturalness" arising from the same qualities in the ancients—particularly Homer, who represented for him the highest literary ideal. Cowper wrote:

> He is the best poet that ever lived for many reasons, but for none more than that majestic plainness that distinguishes him from all others. As an accomplished person moves gracefully without thinking of it, in like manner the dignity of Homer seems to cost him no labour. It was natural to him to say great things, and to say them well, and little ornaments were beneath his notice.

When he began to translate Homer, Cowper attacked Pope with something akin to fury for what Pope had done to a great "natural" genius. He had tied "the bells of rhyme" about Homer's neck, he wrote, ". . . bedizening him with ornament," thus grossly misrepresenting Homer's essential quality of sub-lime simplicity.

Miss Edith Hamilton has repeated Cowper's ideas some-what more explicitly. In *The Greek Way* she writes:

> When Homer says, 'The stars about the bright moon shine clear to see, for no wind stirs the air and mountain

peaks appear and the high headlands' . . . the words so literal, so grave, so unemphatic hardly arrest our attention to see the beauty of them. . . . Birds were birds and nothing else, but how beautiful a thing was a bird. . . . The Greeks were realists, but not as we use the word. They saw the beauty of common things and were content with it.

It was the Greek kind of realism that Cowper himself aspired to achieve. The mountain peak was not in the range of his actual experience; thus he does not try to use it. But he attempts a lesser prospect with an apparent desire for Homeric directness and simplicity:

> now at noon
> Upon the southern side of the slant hills,
> And where the woods fence off the northern blast,
> The season smiles, resigning all its rage,
> And has the warmth of May. The vault is blue
> Without a cloud, and white without a speck
> The dazzling splendour of the scene below.

In a succeeding passage Cowper accurately renders a bird as a bird—by no means the "blithe spirit," disembodied and symbolic, of the Romanticist:

> The redbreast warbles still, but is content
> With slender notes, and more than half suppress'd:
> Pleas'd with his solitude, and flitting light
> From spray to spray where'er he rests he shakes
> From many a twig the pendent drops of ice,
> That tinkle in the wither'd leaves below.

With Cowper's admiration of Homer in mind, we can see then, that his insistence on simplicity of design and language arose out of a classic admiration of the "natural" rather than from any such theory as Wordsworth's in his famous preface to

Lyrical Ballads. This is not to overlook another factor in no
way contradictory. The poet's association with the humble in
his Evangelical religious activities had also influenced him to
feel, it is true, that simplicity in language and living was pref-
erable to the artificiality in both to be found in the urban life
of the time. Thus if the Bible was an important influence—as
it plainly was—on the style, imagery, and content of his poetry,
the simplicity of Biblical style is what Cowper chose to adopt,
not its elements of rich ornamentation and sensuousness. And
his fundamental classical attitude is maintained.

In suggesting the Homeric influence on the style of *The Task*
one does not derogate from the influence of Horace in content
as well as in style. Like Cowper retired in Olney, Horace was
an observer of life from his Sabine farm. Though Cowper
could not sing of wine, women, and song, he did share with
Horace the theme of contentment as well as the gift of being
able to delineate intimately details of daily life; moreover, he
was remarkably able to match much of the balance, maturity,
and manliness in the Latin poet's verse. What is even more
interesting was his discovery of an area of agreement with
Horace by no means generally apparent to his neo-classicist
contemporaries. "Horace," he observed, ". . . cried out a good
many years ago, in the true spirit of poetry, 'How much one
man differs from another!' "

What Cowper saw and commented upon when he looked
out from his "loophole of retreat" were some of the most important humanitarian, social, and political concerns of his
century. Comments on them make Cowper of lasting importance to the historians—who have always been quick to
admire him. But his more essential appeal justly lies in his
direct treatment of concrete situations rather than in his
espousal of general causes. Thus quite plainly the significant
thing is the invitation that he gives his readers to inspect the
retreat itself. And there is an enduring charm about seeing
behind the drawn shutters and closed curtains of the parlor in

the little house on the Market Place in Olney, where of a winter evening Cowper plays Hercules to Mrs. Unwin's Omphale—

> while the bubbling and loud-hissing urn
> Throws up a steamy column, and the cups,
> That cheer but not inebriate, wait on each.

It is all so well known that one hesitates even to mention it again. And so are all the other details of daily interior life ranging from the design of Mrs. Unwin's needlepoint to the menu for the evening supper: "a raddish and an egg." It was a part of Cowper's singularity to achieve a remarkable marriage without the sacrament and without legality or sex. And it is out of the curious resulting ménage that he is able to develop, in the admiring phrase of Sainte-Beuve, a *poésie domestique* of lasting freshness.

Beyond the little parlor was a greenhouse lined with mats and a garden seasonally filled with vegetables and flowers. Here, too, the small world becomes vividly alive. From the perception of singularity in himself, Cowper was remarkably able to see the uniqueness of all the aspects of nature, nothing ever being quite the same—almost everything quiet and undynamic, it is true, but with a being and meaning all its own. And from the conviction that plants and trees have individual existences, he develops an intimacy with growing things that few, if any, had had before him.

Cowper, Mr. Norman Nicholson has observed, was "no poet of the flush and gush of summer, like Hopkins, but one who preferred the quiet days of mid-winter when the world kept still enough for him to watch it." And, we might add, to understand and enjoy it.

Still beyond the garden was the countryside. When Cowper wrote

> For I have lov'd the rural walks through lanes
> Of grassy swarth, close cropt by nibbling sheep

he was expressing the completely sincere sentiments of one of the most inveterate walkers in English literature. Out of his habits as a walker in sunshine, rain, or snow arose his best nature poetry. And he developed a special skill—if I may borrow again from Mr. Nicholson—of making his readers conscious "not only of the thing seen but of the see-er," yet keeping each detached from the other. In reporting directly what he saw, he was able to escape one of the major vices of eighteenth-century descriptive poetry. Thomson, too, had relied on his own observation and often had been most successful with the results. But he was at times so swept away by a contemplation of the great forces of nature animating the universe that he rose to describe what he had not seen. Moreover, Thomson's landscapes—full of accurate detail and three-dimensional though they were—were conscious compositions. And, for all their exact rendering, they were not inevitably localized. Cowper—as I am not the first to observe—is more likely to be impressionistic, rendering details in the order of his becoming aware of them rather than in relation to any preconceived design. For this reason he is most successful not so much in landscapes as in bits of scenes. His photographic accuracy in rendering aspects of locality has caused someone to exclaim, "He is to Buckinghamshire what Cuyp is to Holland."

Thomson, a convert to Deism, glorified Nature as an embodiment of the divine idea. Not so Cowper. In *The Task* he insists, as he had in *Retirement*, that, though Nature bears "the stamp and signature of God," it is not God, nor is it sufficient in itself to reveal God:

> Nature is but a name for an effect,
> Whose cause is God.

This is Cowper speaking as an Evangelical. For purely personal reasons, on the other hand, he arrived at the notion that Nature has a healing power. Equally directly he arrived at the idea that Nature can be a teacher, imparting wisdom beyond the reach of books:

Books are not seldom talismans and spells,
By which the magic art of shrewder wits
Holds an unthinking multitude enthrall'd.

. . . .

But trees, and rivulets whose rapid course
Defies the check of winter, haunts of deer,
And sheep-walks populous with bleating lambs,
And lanes in which the primrose ere her time
Peeps through the moss that clothes the hawthorn root,
Deceive no student.

This begins to sound like Wordsworth, who could indeed have said with Cowper:

Thou know'st my praise of nature most sincere,
And that my raptures are not conjur'd up
To serve occasions of poetic pomp.

But the moral influence, the power to chasten and subdue—as many critics have observed—Cowper does not find in nature. Nor does he feel the mystical power. Again, whereas he knows that natural sights and sounds "lull the spirit while they fill the mind," he finds in them no provocation to thoughts that "lie too deep for tears." Such is a limitation in his imagination—not, however, in his sincerity or his individuality.

There is more than abundant evidence that from the particular quality of Cowper's own suffering arose his compassion for the suffering of others and his ability to transmit that feeling with telling effect. It matters little whether his compassion is for a crazed peasant girl deserted by her sailor lover, the Negro of the "middle passage" whom his fellow man finds "guilty of a skin not colour'd like his own," the poor cottagers hovering over their spare food and meager fires, or the "tim'rous hare" hard pressed in the chase. The remarkable fact is not so much that Cowper is able to express this compassion in moving poetry but that—because of his independence—he was able to escape most of the sentimentalism of his age. He did not subscribe to the idea of the natural goodness of man, for example, or to the Noble Savage cult, one of the pillars of Romantic faith. He was not a pantheist. He rejected the pastoral idealization of rustic life. He was under no illusions about the laziness and worthlessness that at times almost justified the suffering of the poor.

Of himself he writes in one of the best known passages:

> I was a stricken deer, that left the herd
> Long since; with many an arrow deep infixt
> My panting side was charg'd, when I withdrew
> To seek a tranquil death in distant shades.

But, even though he may at moments seem to indulge in the confessional habits ascribed to typical Romanticists, he is chargeable with far less self-pity than either Rousseau or Byron. In the final analysis, he was not sentimental about himself.

In one sense, Cowper is plainly a small poet. At his smallest, he amuses himself with charming little *jeux d'esprit* about cats or dogs or birds or pet hares. On one occasion he apostrophizes an oyster:

> You, shapeless nothing in a dish—
> You that are but almost a fish.

"A letter," he argued—and he had the same feeling about a poem—"may be written upon anything or nothing just as that anything or nothing happens to occur": a visit by a lady-kissing candidate, the rescue of a runaway hare dripping from a tanpit, an old cat in "close conversation" with a garden viper, a "musical" ass, or a balloon ascension that did not come off. The starting point in the expression of his ideas did not matter. It was chiefly the act of communicating that pleased him. For other reasons, too, he ought to have been a small poet, indeed, since he was simply a plump, shy, and amiable little

man who lived in a drab little Buckinghamshire village with
genteel ladies and Evangelical clergymen for his chief com-
panions. He had never been anywhere or done anything. He
had never seen a mountain or a lake. He was even a little
frightened by the Sussex hills. And how, Dr. Johnson might
ask, could one be a poet without ever having seen a mountain?
Or, how, Wordsworth on the other side might ask, could one be
a poet who had never seen a lake?

There is, as E. M. Forster has perceived, a difference between mere smallness of literary subject matter and the perfect
realization and utilization of that smallness. The ability to set
down what one sees or experiences with sincerity, simplicity,
and accuracy is a first-rate artistic gift no matter what the size
of the canvas happens to be. Witness an almost random
example, selected not from the poetry, it is true, but from the
letters and brashly (maybe inexcusably) arranged as if it were
contemporary free verse:

> Mrs. Unwin and I,
> crossing a brook,
> saw from the footbridge
> somewhat at the bottom of the water
> which had the appearance
> of a flower.
>
> Observing it attentively,
> we found
> that it consisted
> of a circular assemblage
> of minnows;
> their heads all met in a centre;
> and their tails
> diverging at equal distances,
> and being elevated
> above their heads

gave them
the appearance of a flower
half blown.

One was longer than the rest;
and as often as a straggler came in sight,
he quitted his place to pursue him,
and having driven him away,
he returned to it again,
no other minnow
offering to take it
in his absence.

This we saw him do
several times.

The object that had attached them all
was a dead minnow
which they all seemed
to be devouring.

This startlingly bare statement without overt comment but
with inherent ironic implications has an unmistakable air of
contemporaneity. It is not quite what Emily Dickinson did in
"A Bird Came Down the Walk," or what Ezra Pound did in "A
Lesson in Aesthetics," or William Carlos Williams in "The
Red Weelbarrow," or Marianne Moore in "The Jerboa," but it
has something of all of them; and it indicates a mastery in the
projection of the commonplace and small that has both re-
spectability and permanence.

There is a danger, on the other hand, of tending to overemphasize Cowper's smallness as a poet, or if not exactly to
overemphasize it at least to present it in the wrong perspective·
Big subjects—epic and tragic—he did not essay, being content
to satisfy his urge for poetic spaciousness in his translation of
Homer. Serious subjects and quite important ones, however,
he did attempt. Canon Overton's assertion that in his own way

Cowper did more for the Evangelical Revival than did either Wesley or Whitefield is ample testimony to Cowper's claim to a demonstrable magnitude in the field of religious verse. The argument that his literary permanence does not rest upon this achievement is another matter.

The underlying irony here—once again and finally—involves the poet's recognition of his singularity, an important part of which resided in his conviction of damnation. When he wrote dull poetry or dull prose, he seemed most often to be under the illusion that he could be saved or, perhaps more accurately, that he owed it to his Evangelical friends to write as if he were capable of salvation. At such times he was likely to assume a piety and an intolerance that ill suited him. In the conviction of damnation, on the other hand, he thought that he was denied a look heavenward, just as he knew that it was not consoling to look inward. So he simply looked about him. And what he saw of beauty and peace he took to himself with quiet delight. What he saw of suffering and pain he took to himself with warm compassion.

It was in his saddest moods, he told William Unwin, that he wrote his most "ludicrous" verse. It was in his least self-consciously pious moods that he wrote his best poetry and prose, the lines in which he reveals with clarity, compactness, and charm the "little" life around him—all he was sure he could hope of heaven.

BIBLIOGRAPHY

OF COWPERIAN STUDIES

1895 to 1960

ABBREVIATIONS

AB—   *American Bookman*
ES—   *Englische Studien*
JEGP—   *Journal of English and Germanic Philology*
MLN—   *Modern Language Notes*
MLQ—   *Modern Language Quarterly*
MLR—   *Modern Language Review*
N&Q—   *Notes and Queries*
PMLA—*Publications of the Modern Language Association*
PQ—   *Philological Quarterly*
RES—   *Review of English Studies*
SP—   *Studies in Philology*
SR—   *Sewanee Review*
SRL—   *Saturday Review of Literature*
TBR—   *New York Times Book Review*
TLS—   *London Times Literary Supplement*

I. BIBLIOGRAPHICAL AIDS

Bateson, F. W., ed. *Cambridge Bibliography of English Literature* (New York: The Macmillan Co., 1941), II, 341-343, and Supplement, V (1927), 421-422. [1]

"Books from the Library of William Cowper," *A Catalogue of Books . . . 1484-1800*, No. 735, Maggs Brothers, Ltd., London, 1944, pp. 90-96.* [2]

    Includes among other items a description of the Cowper family Bible now in the Cowper Museum at Olney. See Appendix A in Wright's *Life*, 1892 ed.

British Museum Catalogue of Printed Books, 1880-1900 (Ann Arbor: J. E. Edwards, 1946), XII, 102-113, and Supplement (1950), III, 62-63. [Reprint] [3]

    The most complete list of British editions.

Brooks, Elmer L. "Cowper's Periodical Contributions," *TLS*, August 17, 1956, p. 487. [4]

    Contributions to the *Arminian Magazine*—particularly "A Tale Founded on Fact" (January 1783) and "The Negro's Complaint" (September 1790). Suggests connection between the Wesleys and Cowper.

Brown, G. A. Bibliography for Chap. IV, "William Cowper," *Cambridge History of English Literature*, edited by Ward and Waller (New York: Putnam, 1914), XI, 444-448. [5]

*Except for a few items of special interest, no attempt has been made to list sales catalogues.

C[hapman], R. W. "A Book from Cowper's Library," *N&Q*, CLXXXVI (June 17, 1944), 291.   [6]

Volume (from the 1943 Sotheby sale) in which Cowper had bound several copies of contemporary periodicals. The purpose of the collection is queried.

Crane, R. S. *et al. English Literature, 1660-1800: A Bibliography of Modern Studies Compiled for Philological Quarterly.* Introduction by Louis A. Landa. 2 vols. (Princeton: Princeton University Press, 1950-52), *passim.*   [7]

Reprint of annual bibliographies in *PQ*, 1925-1950.

Evans, Charles. *American Bibliography* (New York: Peter Smith, 1942), VII-XII. [Reprint]   [8]

For American editions prior to 1800.

Francis, John C. "The Cowper Centenary," *N&Q*, 9th ser., V (April 21, 1900), 301-309.   [9]

A list of "the most interesting" *N&Q* entries to date, together with a biographical sketch of the poet.

Hartley, Lodwick. *William Cowper: a list of critical and biographical studies published from 1895 to 1949* (*North Carolina State College Record*, Vol. XLIX, No. 6) [Raleigh, N. C., February 1950].   [10]

Reviewed by M. J. Quinlan, *PQ*, XXX (1951), 263.

Hodgson, Norma H. [Russell], and Maurice J. Quinlan. "Cowper Again," *MP*, LIII (1956), 213-216.   [11]

Continues the discussion of the Cox and Edwards editions of the autobiography raised by Ryskamp's review of Quinlan's edition of the *Memoir* (139). See also 16.

Leary, Lewis, ed. *Contemporary Literary Scholarship* (New York: Appleton-Century-Crofts, Inc., 1958), 101, 107.   [12]

Comments by James L. Clifford on recent Cowperian scholarship.

Nicholls, Norah. "Early Editions of William Cowper," *Bookman* (London), LXXX (1931), 174.   [13]

See E. G. Crowsley, *ibid.*, 268-269, and Norah Nicholls' reply, 269.—Superficial discussion of Cowper first editions as collector's items, with corrections and rejoinder. Notes price of $500 for a first edition of the *Poems* in the Kern sale in New York.

Povey, Kenneth. "Notes for a Bibliography of Cowper's Letters," *RES*, VII (1931), 182-187; VIII (1932), 316-319; X (1934), 76-78.   [14]

Notes on additions to the text of Cowper's letters published since Wright's *Correspondence*, references to letters and fragments published before publication of the *Correspondence* but not included, notes on the dating of dateless or incorrectly dated letters. See 925.

Ryskamp, Charles. "Cowper and Darwin's *Economy of Vegetation*," *Harvard Library Bulletin*, XI (1957), 317-318.   [15]

Establishes Cowper's authorship of review of Darwin's book in *Analytical Review* in March 1793.

———. "Cowper Once More," *MP*, LIV (1957), 284.   [16]

Further argument on the precedence of the Edwards and Cox editions of the autobiography. Cites letter from John Johnson to Hayley (24 July 1816) describing how Charles Cowper (son of Cowper's cousin, Major William Cowper) tried to keep Edwards from publishing the *Memoir*, which came out on May 4, 1816. See Hodgson and Quinlan (11), Sparrow and Wells (18), Todd (20), and Quinlan (139).

"Sotheby's Sale," *TLS*, May 22, 1943, p. 252.   [17]

Report of sale of books, manuscripts, and relics of Cowper, including corrected proof sheets of the first edition of *Homer*, a manuscript commonplace book, the white linen cap in which the poet was painted by Romney, the buff doeskin waistcoat edged with green silk, and other personal effects owned by Mrs. H. Barham Johnson, widow of the grandson of "Johnny of Norfolk."

Sparrow, John, and John Edwin Wells. "*Memoir of the Early Life of William Cowper* (1816)," *Bibliographical Notes and Queries*, II, No. 3 (April 1936), 7-8; II, No. 6 (July 1936), 3.   [18]

Bibliographical consideration of two slightly divergent copies of the *Memoir* published by Edwards. See 16 and Quinlan (139).

Tobin, James E.   *Eighteenth Century English Literature and Its Cultural Background: A Bibliography* (New York: Fordham University Press, 1939), pp. 94-96.   [19]

Todd, William B.   "On the Use of Advertisements in Bibliographical Studies," *The Library*, 5th ser., VIII (1953), 184.   [20]
     Evidence from review in *British Critic* for July 1816 concerning the rival editions of the *Memoir of the Early Life of William Cowper*.   See 16.

For additional bibliographical aids see the following items: 107, 109, 110, 113, 123, 128, 131, 133, 140, 142, 143, 145, 150, 365, 371, 386, 613, 620, 937.   The reader is further advised to consult the *Annual Bibliography of English Language and Literature*, published by the Modern Humanities Research Association since 1920, the *Year's Work in English Studies*, published by the English Association since 1921, the annual eighteenth-century bibliography published in *Philological Quarterly* [see 7 above], and the annual bibliography in *Publications of the Modern Language Association*.

II. EDITIONS AND SELECTIONS

Adelphi. Cowper Memorials, ed. by H. P. Stokes (Olney: Oliver Ratcliff, at the Cowper Press, 1904), pp. 63-86.   [100]
    Reprint of Cowper's sketch of the character and account of the
last illness of his brother, the Reverend John Cowper, fellow of
Bennet College, Cambridge University, originally published in
1802.

Alden, Raymond M., ed. *Readings in English Prose of the Eighteenth
Century* (Boston: Houghton Mifflin Company, 1911), pp. 525-
533.   [101]

Arber, Edward, ed. *Cowper and His Times* (*English Songs*, v. 10)
(London: Oxford University Press, 1918).   [102]

———, ed. *The Cowper Anthology* (London: Frowde, 1901), pp. 1-
39.   [103]

Bailey, J. C., ed. *The Poems of William Cowper* (London: Methuen,
1905).   [104]
    Text based on the "earliest editions." Biographical and
critical introduction; extensive annotation. Includes 35 letters to
Joseph Hill, John and Catharine Johnson not included by Wright.
—Reviewed *Bookman* (London), XXIX (1906), 39; *Athenaeum*,
No. 4096 (April 28, 1906), 505; *Independent Review*, VIII (1906),
293-305. See 354.

Baillière, Paul, trans. *Poètes allemands et Poètes anglais* (Paris:
Alfonse Lemerre, 1907), pp. 227-239.   [105]
    Includes a translation of "John Gilpin."

Benham, William, ed. *The Poetical Works of William Cowper* (The Globe Edition; London: Macmillan and Company, 1908).   [106]

A reprint of the first edition of 1870. Still useful for its introductory section and its notes.

Bernbaum, Ernest, ed. *Anthology of Romanticism.* (New York: Ronald Press, 1948), 73-80, 1077-1078.   [107]

Cowper as a pre-Romanticist.

Boas, Guy, ed. Selected Poems of *Gray, Collins, Goldsmith, and Cowper* (London and Edinburgh: Thomas Nelson and Sons, [1926]).   [108]

Selections and "contrasts" in the "Teaching of English" series edited by Sir Henry Newbolt.

Bredvold, Louis I., Alan D. McKillop, and Lois Whitney, eds. *Eighteenth Century Poetry and Prose* (New York: The Ronald Press, 1956), pp. 882-935.   [109]

Valuable brief introduction.—"To us [Cowper] is the poet and writer of inimitable letters, who celebrates with a new simplicity and affectionate fidelity to intimate detail the life of retirement in the country."

Bredvold, Louis I., Robert K. Root, and George Sherburn, eds. *Eighteenth Century Prose* (New York: Thomas Nelson and Sons, 1935), pp. 789-804.   [110]

"[Cowper] sees with perfect truth; he thinks and feels with unaffected sincerity. The same qualities make him supreme in the art of the familiar letter." [Introduction.]

Campbell, Kathleen, ed. *An Anthology of English Poetry: Dryden to Blake* (Home University Library; London: Thornton Butterworth, [1930]), pp. 195-209.   [111]

Cecil, Lord David, ed. *Selections from Cowper* (London: Methuen, 1933).   [112]

Crane, Ronald S., ed. *A Collection of English Poems, 1660-1800* (New York: Harper and Brothers, 1932), pp. 952-1005, 1128.   [113]

Useful notes and bibliography.

Davie, Donald, ed. *The Late Augustans* (New York: The Macmillan Company, 1958), pp. xxv-xxvii, 93-98.   [114]

An anthology including "Yardley-Oak" as an example of the poetry of the "late Augustans."

The Diverting History of John Gilpin. Illustrated by Charles E. Brock (New York: E. P. Dutton and Company, 1899).   [115]

———. With wood-cuts by Robert Seaver. (Boston and New York: Houghton Mifflin and Company, 1906).   [116]

———. With drawings by Randolph Caldecott (New York: Frederick A. Stokes, 1925).   See 612, 613.   [117]

———. Illustrated by Jean Emile Laboureur (Paris: R. Davie, 1931).   [Limited Edition]   [118]

———. Illustrated by Ronald Searle (London: Penguin Books, 1953).   [119]

Fausset, Hugh I'Anson, ed. *Poems* (Everyman; London: J. M. Dent, 1931).   [120]

A selection with a brief introduction.—"[Cowper's poetry] was written on the edge of an abyss. It was the frail barrier behind which he strove to preserve all that was gentle, reasonable, and sensitively humane against the demons of madness."—Reviewed in *TLS* ["Power and Gentleness"].   November 19, 1931, pp. 901-902; *Bookman*, LXXXI (1931), 106.   See 378.

Frazer, Sir James G., ed. *Letters of William Cowper.* 2 vols. (London: Macmillan and Company, 1912).   [121]

Text based on Southey.—Contains a lengthy biographical and critical essay as an introduction that, though perpetuating some of the routine anti-Evangelical prejudices and containing no new material, is stimulating and perceptive. Still one of the best brief essays on the poet's life.—Reviewed in *ES*, XLIII (1912), 318; *Blackwood's*, CXCII (1912), 257-262; *Contemporary Review*, CII (1912), 287-290.   See also Starkey (269).

Grebanier, Bernard D., *et al.*, eds. *The Romantic Age* (1760-1832). *[English Literature and Its Background]* (New York: The Dryden Press, 1951), pp. 40-53.   [122]

    " . . . of the pre-romantic poets [Cowper's] influence was the greatest in helping to change the taste of the public in the directions that the nineteenth century was to take." [Introduction.]

Grieve, A. J., ed. *The Task* (Temple Classics; London: J. M. Dent, 1900).   [123]

    Contains a "bibliographical epilogue."

Hadley, William, ed. *Selected Letters* (Everyman; London: J. M. Dent, 1926).   [124]

    Text from Southey.—Reviewed in the *Nation*, CXXIII (1926), 387; *University of California Chronicle*, XXIX (1927), 212.

Homer, *The Odyssey*, trans. by William Cowper. (Everyman; London: J. M. Dent, 1910).   [125]

    Reprinted in 1935. Contains an introduction by F. Melian Stawell, included in the Everyman edition of *The Iliad*, translated by Edward, Earl of Derby.—"[Cowper's] natural brightness, united as it was to perfect delicacy of touch, a delicious humour, and a quivering sensitiveness, rendered him singularly responsive to the clear humanity, tenderness, and depth of the Homeric feeling, and to the charm and vividness of the Homeric fancy."— The text of the first edition is followed.

Jean Gilpin, l'histoire divertissante, etc. . . . . francisée par Eliza Gutch . . . illustrée par Randolph Caldecott. (New York: Frederick A. Stokes, 1925).   [126]

Lucas, E. V., ed. *William Cowper's Letters: A Selection* (World's Classics; London and New York: H. Frowde, 1908).   [127]

    Another edition in 1911 with notes by M. L. Milford. See 921.

Mendenhall, John C., ed. *English Literature, 1650-1800* (Philadelphia: J. B. Lippincott Co., 1940), pp. 953-960.   [128]

    "Cowper's work marks a turn from the notion of the poet as a man active amongst men to the thought of him as a recluse commenting from a distance, busy with his own small interests." [Introduction.]

Milford, [Sir] Humphrey S., ed. *Cowper: Poetry and Prose* (The Clarendon Press Series of English Literature; Oxford: The Clarendon Press, 1921). [129]

Contains introduction and notes. Reprints essays on Cowper by Hazlitt and Bagehot.

————. *The Poetical Works of William Cowper* (Oxford Standard Authors; London: Oxford University Press, 1950). Fourth edition. [130]

The most complete text. Based on royal octavo of 1800. Cf. Bailey (104). First edition, 1905, reprinted 1907. Second edition, 1913; third, 1926; fourth, 1934, reprinted in 1947 and 1950. See 354.

Moore, Cecil A., ed. *English Poetry of the Eighteenth Century* (New York: Henry Holt and Company, 1935), pp. 841-882, 923. [131]

Useful notes and bibliography.

Mumby, Frank Arthur, ed. *Letters of Literary Men* (London: Routledge and Sons, [1906]), I, 318-347. [132]

Selections from the letters.

Murray, James O., ed. *Selections from the Poetical Works of William Cowper* (Athenaeum Press Series; Boston: Ginn and Company, 1898). [133]

Biographical and critical introduction of some merit; notes and bibliography.

New Poems (London: Oxford University Press, 1931). [134]

"Seven poems, six of which are now for the first time printed, while the seventh is from a rare printed broadside and anonymous." From Bod. MS. Eng. misc. d. 135 (a collection made by John Bruce) and a scrap-book owned by Falconer Madan of Oxford.— Reviewed *TLS*, December 3, 1931, p. 986. Reprinted by Milford in the OSA *Cowper*, 1934.

Osgood, Charles G., ed. *The Poetical Works of John Milton . . . Including William Cowper's Translations of the Latin and Italian Poems* (New York: Oxford University Press, 1935). [135]

Poems.   (Augustan Books of Poetry; London: E. Benn, Ltd.,
    1931).   [136]

Poems.   Selected and introduction by Norman Nicholson (Crown
    Classics Series; Grey Walls Press, 1951).   [137]
        See 373.

Poetical Works.   With an introduction by John Bailey (Nelson Poets;
    London: Thomas Nelson Sons, 1925).   [138]

Quinlan, Maurice J., ed.   "Memoir of William Cowper, An Auto-
    biography," *Proceedings of the American Philosophical Society*,
    XCVII (1953), 359-382.   [139]
        In 1816 two editions of the autobiography (neither with the
    above title) were printed in London: one by R. Edwards and the
    other by E. Cox and Son. The Edwards edition with some modern-
    ization is reprinted here. In an introduction, Quinlan argues for
    the precedence of the Cox edition. The argument is challenged by
    Charles Ryskamp in a review in *MP*, LIII (1955), 67-70 (see 16);
    Norma Hodgson and Quinlan reply in *MP*, LIII (1956), 213-216
    (11). Also reviewed by Lodwick Hartley in *PQ*, XXXIII (1954),
    267-268.

Shepard, Odell, and Paul Spencer Wood, eds.   *English Prose and
    Poetry, 1660-1800* (Boston: Houghton Mifflin Company, 1934),
    pp. 866-897, 1055-1058.   [140]
        Critical introduction minimizes Cowper's intellectual courage
    and imaginative penetration, praising chiefly the poet's humor,
    good taste, and intelligence.

Storer, Edward, ed.   *William Cowper* (The Regent Library; Chicago:
    F. W. Browne, 1913).   [141]
        Selections from the poetry and the letters. In the critical in-
    troduction, the editor uses Cowper to belabor the "decadent
    romanticism" of the twentieth century. Regards the poet as a
    classicist chiefly because he employs the natural and ordinary
    rather than the extraordinary. Cf. 324.

Sypher, Wylie, ed. *Enlightened England: An Anthology of Eighteenth Century Literature* (New York: W. W. Norton and Company, 1947), pp. 1020-1047. [142]

Contains brief introduction and bibliography.—"The earth and every common sight are as unpretentiously recorded [in Cowper] as in Wordsworth, but without Wordsworth's contemplative breadth."

Tupper, James Waddell, ed. *English Poems from Dryden to Blake* (New York: Prentice-Hall, 1933), pp. 20, 27-29, 743-789. [143]

"He linked his love of nature with his love of man, and although he could not fuse them in that ecstasy of Wordsworth, he, more than any other poet of the eighteenth century, prepared the way for the great poet of man and nature of the early nineteenth." [Introduction.]

Two Poems Printed in 1798 (Oxford: The Clarendon Press, 1926). [144]

Facsimiles of "On Receipt of My Mother's Picture" and "The Dog and the Water-Lily."

Van Doren, Mark, ed. *The Selected Letters of William Cowper* (New York: Farrar, Straus, and Cudahy, 1951). [145]

Text from Thomas Wright. Introduction and bibliography. Reviewed by Milton Rugoff in *TBR*, September 9, 1951, p. 4; by George Genzmer in *Books* of the New York *Herald-Tribune*, September 2, 1951, p. 5; by Lodwick Hartley in *SRL*, January 5, 1952, pp. 13-14.

Warner, Charles Dudley, *et al.*, eds. *Library of the World's Best Literature* (New York: J. A. Hill and Company, 1896), X, 4107-4116. [146]

Webb, W. T., ed. *Cowper's Shorter Poems* (London: Macmillan and Company, 1896). [147]

Contains useful introduction and notes.

———. *Selections from Cowper's Letters* (London: Macmillan and Company, 1895). [148]

————. *The Task, Book V* (London: Macmillan and Company, 1898). [149]

Useful introduction and notes.

Woods, George Benjamin, ed. *English Poetry and Prose of the Romantic Movement* (Chicago: Scott, Foresman and Company, 1950), pp. 145-154, 1252-1256. [150]

Cowper as a pre-romantic; notes and bibliography.

Wright, Thomas, ed. *The Correspondence of William Cowper.* 4 vols. (London: Hodder and Stoughton, 1904). [151]

Still the most complete edition of the letters, in spite of its many inadequacies. Reviewed *TLS*, April 8, 1904, p. 106; *Athenaeum*, May 14, 1904, pp. 617-619; *Academy*, LXVI (April 16, 1904), 420; *Saturday Review*, XCIX (1905), 12-13; *Quarterly Review*, CCII (1905), 35-60. See 925, 933.

————. *The Unpublished and Uncollected Letters of William Cowper* (London: C. J. Farncombe, 1925). [152]

Reviewed *TLS*, June 25, 1925, p. 428; *New Statesman*, July 25, 1925, pp. 424-425.

————. *The Unpublished and Uncollected Poems of William Cowper* (Cameo Series; London: T. Fischer Unwin, 1900). [153]

III. BIOGRAPHY

A. General

Adcock, Almay St. John, " 'Dear Anonymous,' " *Chamber's Journal,*
8th ser., X (January 1941), 49-52. [200]
    The relationship of Cowper and his cousin Theodora.

Barnard, E. A. B., "Cowper's Mr. Gregson," *N&Q*, CLXXXI (1941),
58. [201]
    Identity of the Throckmorton's chaplain, the Reverend William Gregson, revealed in small memorial on south wall of chancel in Weston Underwood church.

Bentley, Gerald E., Jr. "Blake, Hayley, and Lady Hesketh," *RES,*
XXVII (1956), 264-268. [202]
    Correspondence between Hayley and Lady Hesketh regarding Blake's engraving of Cowper's portrait for Hayley's *Life.* See Fairchild (226) and Keynes (433).

Bishop, Morchard. *Blake's Hayley: The Life, Works and Friendships of William Hayley* (London: Gollancz, 1951), *passim.* [203]
    Particularly valuable for the treatment of Cowper's last decade and for the story of Hayley's biography of Cowper. See 202, 211, 222, 438.

Blyton, W. J. "A Puritan's Catholic Friends: Cowper and the Throckmortons," *The Month,* CLXIX (March 1937), 218-224. [204]
    See 214 and 399.

Bolton, Sir William. "The Poet Cowper and His Surroundings," *Transactions of the Royal Society of Literature of the United Kingdom*, 2nd ser., XXII (1901), 133-164. [205]

A highly discursive essay on the way in which the village of Olney reflects the life and poetry of Cowper. Includes, among other things, an account (based on the diary of Lady Mary Cowper, wife of Earl Cowper, the Chancellor) of the way in which the office of Clerk of the Parliaments came into the possession of the Cowper family. Appendices print originals of letters to Clotworthy Rowley of February 21, 1788, and to William Hayley of November 25, 1792, and reproduce the Cowper book-plate with a note on the way it differs from the poet's engraved seal.

Bradford, Gamaliel. "Diversions of a Lost Soul," *Atlantic Monthly*, CXXXIV (1924), 361-370. [206]

Also included in Bradford's *Bare Souls* (New York and London: Harper and Brothers, 1924), pp. 135-168.—Concerns Cowper's preoccupation with the idea of damnation.

Bridgewater, William, and Eliza J. Sherwood, eds. "William Cowper," *The Columbia Encyclopedia* (New York: Columbia University Press, 1952), Second Edition, p. 472. [207]

Brookfield, Frances M. *The Cambridge 'Apostles'* (New York: Charles Scribner's Sons, 1906), p. 263. [208]

James Spedding's statement to William Bodham Donne concerning Southey's hint that some "very strange" information about Cowper would not be made public. See 230.

Brown, Wallace C. *Charles Churchill: Poet, Rake, and Rebel* (Lawrence: University of Kansas Press, 1953), 11-13, 63-65. [209]

Relationship between Cowper and Churchill at Westminster and in the "Nonsense Club." See 265.

Cairns, William T. "John Newton: A Vindication," *The Religion of Dr. Johnson and Other Essays* (London: Oxford University Press, 1946), pp. 24-57. [210]

Concerned chiefly with the Newton-Cowper relationship.

Caldicott, H. R. S. "How Cowper Got His Pension: A Study in Minute History from a Manuscript by William Hayley," *Cornhill Magazine*, CVII (1913), 493-507. [211]

Hayley's efforts in Cowper's behalf. See 203 and 222.

Callis, The Rt. Rev. John, *et al. John Newton, Sailor, Preacher, Pastor and Poet, Centenary Memorials* (London: S. W. Partridge and Company, 1908). [212]

Biographical materials on Cowper's most influential Evangelical friend. See Martin (249).

Carmichael, Montgomery. "Cowper's Friends," *Catholic World*, CXXXIV (1932), 456-466. [213]

A discussion of Mrs. Unwin, Lady Hesketh, and the Reverend John Johnson ("Johnny of Norfolk"), based chiefly on Catharine Bodham Johnson's edition of the *Letters of Lady Hesketh* (237).

———. "William Cowper and the Throckmortons," *Dublin Review*, CXC (1932), 195-210. [214]

Cowper's Catholic friends at Weston.

Cecil, Lord David. *The Stricken Deer, or The Life of Cowper* (London: Constable, 1929). [215]

Reprinted in the World's Classics Series (New York: Oxford University Press, 1930).—Reviewed *TLS*, December 19, 1929, p. 1077; *SRev*, CXLVIII (1929), 727; *Nation and Athenaeum*, XLVI (1929), 13, 461; *Spectator*, December 28, 1929, pp. 981-982; *New Statesman*, XXIV (1929), 371; *Yale Review*, XX (1929), 403-405; *Year's Work in English Studies*, X (1929), 306; *Criterion*, IX (1930), 545-548; *London Mercury*, XXI (1930), 565-567; *AB*, LXXI (1930), 333-334; *SRL*, VI (May 10, 1930), 1026-1027; *New Republic*, LXIV (1930), 105-106; *Nation*, CXXX (1930), 708-709.

Chapman, Edward Mortimer. "One Hundred Years After," *Outlook*, LXIV (1900), 918-921. [216]

A centenary essay, with a comparison of Cowper and Southey.

Church, Leslie F. "The Madness of Cowper," *London Quarterly and Holborn Review*, CLXI (1936), 102-104. [217]

An editorial supporting Gilbert Thomas' treatment of the poet's melancholy. See 278; also 221.

Cowper in London. Papers Read before the Cowper Society (London: Everett and Co., 1907). [218]

Papers by John Sargeaunt (265), Frederick Rogers (262), and Lucius Fry (607) listed separately. Contains a prefatory account of the meetings of the Cowper Society with programs from 1901 to 1906.

"Cowper's House at Olney," *Bookman*, XI (1900), 410. [219]

Picture of the house, now Cowper Museum, with a note on the Centennial celebration. See 242.

"Cowper's Last Years," *TLS*, October 5, 1951, p. 636, and October 12, 1951, p. 652. [220]

Reprints copy of John Johnson's diary presumably copied from original in the Swarthmore College library, reprinted in *PMLA*, XLII (1927), 946-962 (268). This MS gives a pointer to another part of the diary now in the Cambridge University Library (MS. Add. 6755G) from which T. R. Glover made a transcript (Cambridge MS. Add. 5993).—The account of Cowper's dreams and voices between November 15, 1797, and April 23, 1799. See 220.

"Cowper's Sanity Was Saved by His Religion," *Christian Century*, XLVIII (1931), 1645-1646. [221]

An editorial contending that the poet's "faith was far more of an antidote to the insanity which always threatened him than a cause of it." See 217.

Dowden, Edward. "Cowper and William Hayley," *Atlantic Monthly*, C (1907), 74-87. [222]

Account of Hayley's effort to get pension for Cowper and his scheme for alleviating the poet's mental distress.—Reprinted in *Essays Modern and Elizabethan* (New York: Dutton, 1910). See 211.

Dunelm, Handley. "A Tradition of Cowper's Death," *TLS*, January 11, 1918, p. 21. [223]

The account of the "happy death" of Cowper as presumably related by John Johnson to William Marsh (1775-1864).

Elwin, Whitwell. "Cowper," *Some Eighteenth-Century Men of Letters* (London: John Murray, 1902), I, 370-508. [224]

A revision and expansion of an article published in the *Quarterly Review* in January 1860 into a biography unfinished at the time of the author's death.

Fairchild, Hoxie Neale. "Additional Notes on John Johnson's Diary," *PMLA*, XLIII (1928), 571-572. [225]

A reply to Spiller (268). See also 220.

———. "Unpublished References to Blake by Hayley and Lady Hesketh," *SP*, XXV (1928), 1-10. [226]

Correspondence regarding Hayley's *Life* and Blake's illustrations. Cites two volumes of MS letters (BM. Add. MS. 30, 803) containing "much unused material on Cowper." Concerns Lady Hesketh's objection to Blake's engraving of the Romney portrait as a "horrible representation" of "our angelic friend." See Bentley (202).

Fausset, Hugh I'Anson. *William Cowper* (London: Jonathan Cape, 1928). [227]

Reviewed *TLS*, October 25, 1928, p. 776; *Nation and Athenaeum*, XLIV (1928), 5, 180; *New Statesman*, XXXII (1928), 16; *SRL*, CXLVI (October 27, 1928), 543; *Year's Work in English Studies*, IX (1928), 280-281; *AB*, LXIX (1929), 205.

Geary, Caroline. *Cowper and Mary Unwin, A Centenary Memento* (London: Henry J. Drane [1901?]). [228]

An outgrowth of the Cowper centenary celebration at Olney, aptly characterized by the author as "a labour of love" tracing "the vague and melancholy episode of the poet's love story." A sentimentalized account employing local tradition as the only fresh source of material.

Gore-Browne, Robert. *Chancellor Thurlow* (London: Hamilton, 1953), pp. 238-239, 301-303, 307-312, and *passim*. [229]

Relationship of Cowper and his friend of Westminster days. See 265.

Greville, Charles Cavendish Fulke. *Memoirs 1814-1860*, ed. by Lytton Strachey and Roger Fulford (London: Macmillan and Company, 1938), III, 85.   [230]

Unexpurgated version of the famous memoirs, containing reference to a rumored physical defect of Cowper. See Fairchild (334), Gregory (296), Quinlan (257), and Ryskamp (263).

Hannay, Neilson Campbell. "The Religious Element in the Life and Character of William Cowper," Harvard University dissertation, 1919. [Unpublished.]   [231]

In the religious life and views of Cowper, there was, in spite of his recurrent malady, a certain development from a period of unrestrained pietism to a state of breadth, tolerance, and poise. See Thein (278), Lanham (359), and Possehl (377).

Hartley, Lodwick. "Cowper and the Evangelicals: Notes on Early Biographical Interpretations," *PMLA*, LXV (1950), 719-731. [232]

The beginnings of the biographical controversy regarding the relation of religion to Cowper's madness.

Hooper, Wilfred. "Cowper and the Temple," *The Times* (London), November 27, 1931, p. 14.   [233]

Newspaper account of an address at a public meeting of the Cowper Society in Middle Temple Hall on November 26, 1931. Attempts to determine Cowper's successive places of residence first in the Middle Temple and later in the Inner Temple. See Ryskamp (263), pp. 64-77.

———. "Cowper's 'Sephus,'" *N&Q*, 12th ser., V (October, 1919), 258-259.   [234]

Biographical sketch of Cowper's friend and correspondent, Joseph Hill.

Hunt, Alfred Leedes. *Evangelical By-Paths* (London: Thynne and Company, 1927), p. 89.   [235]

The rumor, reported by the Reverend David Simpson (curate to William Unwin) that "Cowper's first derangement was occasioned by a love affair with the kept mistress of Lord Thurlow."

Hunt, R. N. Carew. "John Newton and William Cowper," *Nineteenth Century and After*, CXXX (1941), 92-96. [236]
A routine defense of Newton.

Johnson, Catharine Bodham [Mrs. H. Barham]. "Lady Hesketh and 'Johnny of Norfolk'" *Monthly Review*, III (June 1901), 151-162. [237]
The letters of Lady Hesketh to John Johnson between 1784 and 1800, particularly as they reflect her own character ("a somewhat fussy old lady . . . reigning like a little queen at Bath"), her concern for the welfare of Cowper, her inclination to grudge the rest of the world any share in her cousin's affections, her unflattering view of Mrs. Unwin, her fears of the French Revolution, and her connections with the Court.

————, ed. *Letters of Lady Hesketh to the Reverend John Johnson* (London: Jarrold and Sons, 1901). [238]

————. *William Bodham and His Friends* (New York: Dutton, 1905), *passim*. [239]
Cowper's family relations on his maternal side.

King, T. H. "Cowper's Mother and an Early Lover," *N&Q*, CXLII (September 6, 1924), 167. [240]
Ann Donne Cowper's early engagement to Samuel Hudson of Great Yarmouth, Norfolk, and Leghorn, Italy.

Law, Alice. "William Cowper," *Fortnightly Review*, LXVII (1900), 755-779. [241]
A centenary essay mainly concerned with "the vexed question of Newton's influence over Cowper."

Lea, C. H. "Cowper's House at Olney," *AB*, LXXXI (1931), 106. [242]
Brief description of the interior of the house (now Cowper Museum) with photograph of the sofa. See 219.

Mack, Edward C. *Public Schools and British Opinion, 1780-1860* (New York: Columbia University Press, 1938), pp. 17-18. [243]
Cowper and his schoolmates at Westminster. See 265.

MacKinnon, Sir F. D. "Dr. Johnson and the Temple," *Cornhill Magazine*, N. S. LVII (1924), 470-471.   [244]

Proximity of Samuel Johnson's lodgings and Cowper's in the Temple in 1763.   See Ryskamp (263), p. 74.

M[acPike], E. F.   "William Cowper and John Johnson," *N&Q*, CLXXXIII (December 5, 1942), 351-352 and CLXXXV (December 18, 1943), 385.   [245]

Miscellaneous notes on the family of Cowper's "Johnny of Norfolk" by a contributor who makes and answers his own queries. See entries below.

————. "William Cowper's Godson," *N&Q*, CLXXXIII (August 15, 1942), 117-188.   [246]

See also *ibid.*, pp. 18 and 111.—Identified as William Cowper Rose, son of Samuel Rose.

————. "William Hayley and John Johnson," *N&Q*, CLXXXIII (August 15, 1942), 110.   [247]

See above.

Magill, Frank N., and Dayton Kohler, eds.   "William Cowper," *Cyclopedia of World Authors* (New York: Harper and Brothers, 1958), pp. 250-251; and (New York: Salem Press, 1958), II, 250-251.   [248]

Martin, Bernard.   *John Newton* (London: Heinemann, 1950).   [249]

The definitive biography of Cowper's friend.   See review by M. J. Quinlan, *PQ*, XXX (1951), 242-243.

May, George Lacey.   *Some Eighteenth Century Churchmen* (London: Society for Promotion of Christian Knowledge, 1920).   [250]

A critical-biographical essay contending that "as a mirror of contemporary thought and religion, [Cowper's life] is full of interest for a modern reader," that the long poems, though containing many beautiful passages "are too obviously didactic to be works of art," that letter-writing is the art in which he really excelled.

Norman, Herbert J. "The Melancholy of Cowper," *Westminster Review*, CLXXV (1911), 638-647. [251]

A study of the many reasons assigned to Cowper's madness, concluding that "Cowper was the victim of some inborn defect of nerve tissue, that which predisposed him to attacks of melancholia." Cf. 295 and 297.

Povey, Kenneth. "The Banishment of Lady Austen," *RES*, XV (1939), 392-400. [252]

Argues that the break between Cowper and Lady Austen was by mutual agreement and occasioned no violent or bitter feelings. See 287.

———. "Cowper and Lady Austen," *RES*, X (1934), 417-427. [253]

Transcript of confidential memoranda on Lady Austen now in Fitzwilliam Museum, Cambridge, addressed to William Hayley by the Reverend Samuel Greatheed. Presents Lady Austen as a somewhat plain Evangelical lady of a vivacity not always acceptable.

———. "Cowper's Spiritual Diary," *London Mercury*, XV (1927), 493-496. [254]

Fragmentary diary written by Cowper in 1795 immediately before he left Weston Underwood for Norfolk. Printed from a copy in the hand of John Johnson. For corrections see *ibid.*, p. 640.

Probart, G. Carwardine. "'The Stricken Deer,'" *N&Q*, CLVIII (May 31, 1930), 381-382. [255]

Letter from Hayley to Thomas Carwardine describing conditions at Weston in 1794.

Quinlan, Maurice J. "An Intermediary between Cowper and [Samuel] Johnson," *RES*, XXIV (1948), 141-147. [256]

Suggests Benjamin Latrobe, Moravian minister.

———. *William Cowper: A Critical Life* (Minneapolis: University of Minnesota Press, 1953). [257]

Reviewed by P. Farjeix, *Études Anglaises*, VIII (1953), 263-265; James L. Clifford, *SRL*, XXXVI (April 4, 1953), 32; *U. S. Quarterly Book Review*, IX (June 1953), 121; Edith J. Morley,

Year's Work in English Studies, XXIV (1953), 231-232; W. H. Irving, *SAQ*, LII (1953), 473-475; Lodwick Hartley, *MLN*, LXIX (1954), 125-128; Charles Ryskamp, *PQ*, XXXIII (1954), 268-269.

――――. "William Cowper and the French Revolution," *JEGP*, L (1951), 483-490.   [258]

Attempts to reconcile the revolutionary sentiment in the sonnet to Richard Phillips and the loyalist propaganda in the ballad, "A Good Song," to the general background of Cowper's reaction to the French Revolution. Cf. 327.

――――. "William Cowper and the Unpardonable Sin," *Journal of Religion*, XXIII (1943), 110-116.   [259]

Denies that Cowper's religious melancholy stemmed from Evangelical contacts. (Most of this material is included in 257 above.)

Reed, Myrtle. *Love Affairs of Literary Men* (New York and London: G. P. Putnam's Sons, 1907), pp. 87-105.   [260]

A popular novelist treats the story of Cowper and Mary Unwin.

Ridley, H. M. "Great Friendships: William Cowper and Mrs. Unwin," *Canadian Magazine*, LIX (1922), 438-442.   [261]

Rogers, Frederick. "Cowper in the Temple," *Cowper in London, Papers Read before the Cowper Society* (London: Everett, 1907). [262]

A lively account of the Temple in the poet's day, his residence there, his social life, and his early publications (especially the *Connoisseur* essays) as they reflect on his life. See 263.

Ryskamp, Charles. *William Cowper of the Inner Temple, Esq.* (Cambridge: Cambridge University Press, 1959).   [263]

A study of the poet's life and works to 1786. Appendices include uncollected letters and essays, uncollected poems, and un-collected contributions to magazines.—Reviewed in *Johnsonian News Letter*, XIX (June 1959), 3-4; by Kenneth Young in *Daily Telegraph* (London), June 26, 1959, p. 15; in *Times* (London), July 2, 1959, p. 9; by D. D. in *New Statesman*, LVIII (August 8,

1959), 171-172; by Rosemary Rendel in *Time and Tide*, XL (August 8, 1959), 851; by J. R. in *The Observer*, August 9, 1959, p. 10; *TLS*, August 21, 1959, p. 478; *The Economist*, August 29, 1959, pp. 633-634; by David Rees in the *Manchester Weekly Guardian*, September 17, 1959, p. 11. See 937.

Sargeaunt, John. *Annals of Westminster School* (London: Methuen, 1898), pp. 165-188. [264]

Cowper's schooling under John Nicoll.—"Cowper . . . is himself a sufficient example to prove that Westminster training could in itself make a man of letters." See below.

―――――. "Cowper's School Days in Westminster," *Cowper in London, Papers Read before the Cowper Society* (London: Everett, 1907). [265]

A fuller account than the one in reference above, utilizing essentially the same materials.—"As a theologian [Cowper] might calumniate the public school, but as a man of feeling and honour, as a man of letters and learning, he never lost his affection and reverence for the school where he himself was bred." See 209, 229, 243, 809.

Shorter, Clement K. *Highways and Byways in Buckinghamshire* (London: Macmillan and Company, 1910), pp. 313-333. [266]

Description of Cowper's Olney and environs.

―――――. "William Cowper," *Encyclopaedia Britannica*, 11th ed. (Cambridge: Cambridge University Press, 1910), VII, 349-351. [267]

Spiller, Robert E. "A New Biographical Source for William Cowper," *PMLA*, XLII (1927), 946-962. [268]

The diary of the Reverend John Johnson ("Johnny of Norfolk") in the Swarthmore College library. See reply by Fairchild (225) and "Cowper's Last Years" (220).

[Starkey, James.] "Cowper and Newton," *Essays and Recollections, by Seumas O'Sullivan* (Dublin and Cork: Talbot Press, 1944), pp. 38-47. [269]

An argument in support of the contention of Frazer (121) and others that Newton was the "principal cause" of Cowper's mental disorder, based on the study of the fourteenth letter in Newton's *Twenty-six Letters on Religious Subjects* (London, 1774)—the addressee of which, according to a marginal notation in Starkey's copy (presumably made by one "John Foster" in 1777), was the poet.

Stauffer, Donald A. *The Art of Biography in the Eighteenth Century* (Princeton: Princeton University Press, 1941), pp. 303-307. [270]

    Cowper's *Memoir* as "the flowering into art of the evangelical autobiographies of God's mercies . . . In no biography has the terror of desolation been more perfectly recorded than in Cowper's account of his early life."

Stephen, Sir Leslie. "William Cowper," *Dictionary of National Biography* (London: Oxford University Press, 1938), IV, 1319-1327. [271]

Stokes, Henry Paine. *Cowper Memorials* (Olney: Oliver Ratcliff, at the Cowper Press, 1904). [272]

    Published "at the request of members of the Cowper Society," contains a life of John Cowper, a reprint of *Adelphi*, a "literary history" of the Cowper family, and a genealogy of the family, together with several appendices containing letters of and relating to John Cowper and poems by him. See 100.

Sylvan, Urbanus [Henry Charles Beeching]. "Conference on Books and Men. XIII. William Cowper," *Cornhill Magazine*, LXXXI (1900), 694-701. [273]

    Reprinted in *Living Age*, CCXXV (1900), 552-558.—Chiefly a brief rehearsal of "Cowper's legend," with special emphasis on "the influences that determined his devotion to literature." Contends that Cowper's appeal is still fresh and that his poetry is, therefore, truly "classical."

Symington, Andrew J. *The Poet of Home Life: Centenary Memories of William Cowper.* (London: "Home Words" Office [1900]). [274]

    A disjointed and discursive essay on the life and works, quoting extensively from the letters and the poetry and generously illustrated with photographs and engravings. The volume also includes two centenary sermons ("The Poet of Home," preached by the Very Reverend F. W. Farrar, Dean of Canterbury, at Olney, on April 25, 1900, and "Cowper's Religion," preached by the Rev. John Callis at the East Dereham Church, Norfolk, on the same date), miscellaneous essays ("Cowper's Tame Hare" by the Reverend Canon Wilton, "Cowper's Hymnody," and "The History of John Gilpin" by the Rev. Charles Bullock), and a description of the centenary celebration at Olney.

Tarver, J. C. "Cowper's Ouse," *Macmillan's Magazine*, LXXXII (1900), 135-142.   [275]

Reprinted in *Living Age*, CCXXVI (1900), 158-167. A centenary study of the surroundings of the poet at Olney.

Terhune, Mary Virginia (Hawes) [Marion Harland]. *William Cowper* (New York and London: Putnam, 1899).   [276]

The second biography in a series called *Literary Hearthstones* and subtitled "Studies of the Home Life of Certain Writers and Thinkers." A valueless popular study sentimentalizing the gentle, home-keeping poet and his tragedy.—Reviewed in *The Nation*, LXIX (November 16, 1899), 380; *The Literary World*, XXX (November 25, 1899), 403-404; *The Dial*, XXVII (December 1, 1899), 429; *Athenaeum*, No. 3777 (March 17, 1900), 333.

Thein, Adelaide E. "The Religion of John Newton," *PQ*, XXI (1942), 146-170.   [277]

Counters Gilbert Thomas's (280) contention that Newton's Calvinism was either "mild" or "relatively innocuous." Returns in part to Fausset's view (227).

———. "The Religion of William Cowper, An Attempt to Distinguish His Obession and His Creed," *Microfilm Abstracts*, V, No. 1 (1943), 24-25. (Abstract of University of Michigan Dissertation.)   [278]

Argues that Cowper's obsession and his considered beliefs were separate and arose from different sources. His creed tends toward the ethical and social emphases of enlightened Anglicanism. See 231 and 359.

———. "William Cowper," *New Century Cyclopedia of Names*, edited by Clarence L. Barnhart and William D. Halsey (New York: Appleton-Century-Crofts, Inc., 1954), I, 1114.   [279]

Thomas, Gilbert. *William Cowper and the Eighteenth Century* (London: Nicholson and Watson, 1935). Another edition [only slightly revised], 1949. [280]

Reviewed in *TLS*, September 5, 1935, p. 549; *Spectator* CLV (September 6, 1935), 362; *Fortnightly Review*, CXLIV (1935), 506-507; *London Mercury*, XXXII (1935), 597-598; *ES*, LXXI (1937), 413-415; *TBR*, July 10, 1949, p. 21; *Contemporary Review*, LLXXVI (1949), 190-191. See also *PQ*, XXIX (1950), 270-271, and *MLN*, LXVI (1951) 57-59.

Todd, William B. "Cowper's Commentary on the *Life of Johnson*," *TLS*, March 15, 1957, p. 168. [281]

Comments on the *Life* made by Cowper to John Johnson and recorded by him in his copy of the second edition (1793), now owned by Mr. Todd. Though Cowper was in his last years when the book was read to him, his comments are rational and composed.

Trent, William P. "William Cowper," *Encyclopedia Americana* (New York and Chicago: Americana Corporation, 1947), VIII, 136-138. [282]

Westacott, Charles Albert. *William Cowper, The Animal's Poet Laureate* (Letchworth, Herts: Westacott, 1946). [283]

A pamphlet in a series of studies of representative English poets "who have observed closely the ways of Nature and have experienced a universal kinship with Animals and Birds."

Whiting, Mary Bradford. " 'A Burning Bush': A New Light on Relations between William Cowper and John Newton," *Hibbert Journal*, XXIV (1926), 303-313. [284]

A MS account by Hannah Jowett of Newton's funeral sermon on Cowper. See below.

———. "Cowper and Newton," *Nation* (London), XLVIII (1930), 43-44. [285]

Another reference to Newton's funeral sermon using Hannah Jowett's MS book to correct reference in Newton's letter to Hannah More, written in May 1800, from Eccl. ii., 2, 3, to Exod. iii., 2, 3. See above.

Willis, William. *Cowper and His Connection with the Law* (Norwich: C. G. Gallpen, Printer [1910]). [286]

A paper read at the annual meeting of the Cowper Society in Old Hall, Lincoln's Inn, April 26, 1910. Demonstrates that references in all biographies up to and including Wright's treat Cowper's years in the Middle and Inner Temple with insufficient examination of the evidence. Cites entries on the Rolls of both the Inns of Court to establish the actual facts. See 263.

Woolf, Virginia. "Cowper and Lady Austen," *Nation and Athenaeum*, XLV (1929), 793-795. [287]

Reprinted in *The Second Common Reader* (New York: Harcourt, Brace and Company, 1932), pp. 150-158.—Contends that Cowper's mania regarding damnation and not Mrs. Unwin's jealousy was the ultimate cause of the rift between Cowper and Lady Austen. Cf. Povey (252 and 253).

Wright, G. W. "William Cowper and the Quakers," *N&Q*, CXCVI (1951), 368. [288]

Cites a passage in "a manuscript diary" (not further identified) which refers to "very extensive gatherings illustrating the Life of the Poet Cowper" by a Quaker named Thomas Thompson.

Wright, John. "Famous Visitors of the Eighteenth Century: William Cowper," *Sussex County Magazine*, XX (February and March, 1946), 30-34, 60-65. [289]

Wright, Thomas. *The Life of William Cowper* (London: Farncombe, 1921). [290]

A second edition (first edition, 1892) with extensive revisions and new material. With all its faults, this biography is still valuable.

————, ed. *The Diary of Samuel Teedon, 17 October 1791 to 2 February 1794* (London [O. Ratcliff, printer, Olney] 1902). [291]

B. MEDICAL AND PSYCHOLOGICAL STUDIES

Boutin, Jean, M. D. *Étude Médico-Psychologique sur William Cowper* (Lyon: Rey, 1913). [295]

Cowper is treated as a melancholic whose madness was confined to his religious ideas. Psychological reasons are assigned to the breakdowns with an underlying organic cause, diagnosed as chronic nephritis, giving rise to a uraemia with a toxic effect on the system.

Gregory, Hoosag K. "The Prisoner and His Crimes: A Psychological Approach to the Life and Writings of William Cowper," Harvard University dissertation, 1951. [Unpublished.]   [296]
    See below.

———. "The Prisoner and His Crimes: Summary Comments on a Longer Study of the Mind of William Cowper," *Literature and Psychology*, VI (May 1956), 53-59.   [297]
    Examines Cowper's Oedipal phase of development, discusses effect of possible genital deformity, presents the poet as walking "a straight and narrow asexual path between the chasms of masculinity and femininity," detects an "unintegrated dichotomy" in the poetry between "subjective communications of his deeper problems and Horatian attempts to describe experiences attractive to the normal sensibility and easily accessible to it."

Lloyd, James Hendrie. "The Case of William Cowper, the English Poet," *Archives of Neurology and Psychiatry*, XXIV (1930), 682-689.   [298]
    A routine and superficial treatment of the poet as a manic-depressive, based on an inadequate examination of primary materials. Diagnoses his disease as "a form of circular insanity, with alternating phases of profound and mild hypomanic reaction . . . a constitutional psychosis."

Rosanoff, Aaron Joshua. *Manual of Psychiatry and Mental Hygiene* (New York: John Wiley and Sons, 1938), pp. 593-601.   [299]
    Cowper as a classic example of the "so-called manic depressive psychosis." The *Memoir* (139) is used as case-history.

IV. CRITICISM

A. GENERAL

Ainger, Alfred. "Cowper," *Lectures and Essays* (London: Macmillan and Company, 1905), I, 273-299.   [300]

Cowper as a leader in the "poetic revival of 1760-1820."

Arrieta, Rafael Alberto. *Estudios en tres literaturas* (Buenos Aires: Editorial Losada, s.a. [1939]).   [301]

Includes "Un poeta rural inglés del siglo XVIII [Guillermo Cowper]," reprinted from *Humanidades*, XXII (La Plata, 1934), 33-46.

Atkins, J. W. H. *English Literary Criticism, 17th and 18th Centuries* (New York: Barnes and Noble, Inc., 1950), 219-224.   [302]

"Cowper's critical contribution is by no means negligible, but is full of significant pronouncements."

Bagehot, Walter. "William Cowper," *Estimations in Criticism*, edited by Cuthbert Lennox (London: Andrew Melrose, 1908), I, 40-101.   [303]

Reprint of an essay that first appeared in the *National Review* for July 1855.—"There is no writer more exclusively English. There is no one—or hardly one perhaps—whose excellencies are more natural to our soil, and seem so little able to bear transplantation."

Battenhouse, Henry M. "William Cowper," *English Romantic Writers* (Great Neck, N. Y.: Barron's Educational Series, 1958), 41-45.   [304]

"... in the list of those in whom a certain childlike quality of innocence is associated with a mature and vivid perception of objects in their primary power to heal and inform the human spirit, [Cowper] is among the first of our English poets."

Baugh, Albert C., *et al.* *A Literary History of England* (New York and London: Appleton-Century-Crofts, Inc., 1948), pp. 1096-1102.   [305]

"[Cowper] is like his favorite beverage, at best cheering, never inebriating." [George Sherburn.]

Bayne, Thomas. "Southey on Cowper," *N&Q*, 9th ser., VI (August 4, 1900), 88.   [306]

In a letter of 1809 Southey expressed the idea that Cowper's "popularity is owing to his piety, and that that piety is craziness."

Beaty, Anna Leahy. "Nature and William Cowper," *Dissertations Accepted for Higher Degrees in the Graduate School*, Fordham University, March, 1936, p. 48. (Abstract of unpublished Master's thesis.)   [307]

Cowper's intimate, though limited, knowledge of nature and the three-fold interpretation of nature in his poetry: "as human simplicity, as scenic beauty, and as the manifestation of God's creative power." See 347.

Bernbaum, Ernest. *Guide Through the Romantic Movement* (New York: Ronald Press, 1949), pp. 22-23.   [308]

Cowper as a pre-romantic and as a pleasing example of eighteenth-century sentimentalism.

Birrell, Augustine. "William Cowper," *Living Age*, CCXXV (1900), 391-394.   [309]

Reprinted from *The Leisure Hour*. See *Review of Reviews*, XXI (1900), 610.—Cowper's initial reputation as "the favorite poet of Protestant piety," the eclipse of that reputation during the period of the great Romantics, and his re-emergence as a "prince of prose" with the publication of the letters in 1836.

Blunden, Edmund. "William Cowper: Harmonist of the Country-side," *Times* (London), 13 November 1931, pp. 15-16.   [310]

A bi-centenary appreciation.—"As a harmonist of country life . . . Cowper may be even more beloved in the future than he is now . . . he has succeeded in being our most natural interpreter, perhaps, of the things we go out to see . . . Standing apart he was the reverse of indifferent . . . his placidity of surface was co-existent with a deep energy; he devoted himself to the noblest and the sweetest in human nature so far as he might express them."

Booth, Edward Townsend. "William Cowper: Oh for a Lodge," *God Made the Country* (New York: A. A. Knopf, 1946), pp. 147-149.   [311]

An appreciation of Cowper as a poet of country life in the classical tradition.

Brash, W. B. "William Cowper, 1731-1931," *London Quarterly Review*, CLVI [5th ser. XLIII] (1931), 159-169.   [312]

A bi-centenary appreciation of Cowper's "charm," borrowing heavily from Lord David Cecil's biography.

Brooke, Stopford A. *Naturalism in English Poetry* (New York: E. P. Dutton and Company, 1920), pp. 99-112.   [313]

"From [Cowper's] work, as from a railway station, issued a number of new lines on which the engines of the new poetry ran to varied goals."

Brown, Wallace C. *The Triumph of Form. A Study of the Later Masters of the Heroic Couplet* (Chapel Hill: University of North Carolina Press, 1948), pp. 132-141.   [314]

Cowper's heroic couplet was freer and more relaxed than that of Pope and Johnson. Although his own couplets "were broadly within the neo-classic tradition, his critical view . . . is strikingly like that of Keats and Leigh Hunt." Cf. 387.

Brown, Winifred Elsie May. *The Polished Shaft; Studies in the Purpose and Influence of the Christian Writer in the Eighteenth Century.* London: Society for Promotion of Christian Knowledge, 1950 [1951].   [314a]

Contains essays on William Cowper, William Gilpin, and James Hervey.

Bush, Douglas. *Science and English Poetry* (New York: Oxford University Press, 1950), pp. 76-78. [315]

"[Cowper] praises science united with religion, but he denounces vain measurements and pretensions of unbaptized science." See 358.

Carmichael, Montgomery. "William Cowper (1731-1931)," *Catholic World*, CXXXXIV (1931), 137-148. [316]

A bi-centenary appreciation of the poet as "by far the most attractive, impressive and sympathetic figure among the illustrious insane."

Cavit, T. E. "A Plea for Cowper," *Gentleman's Magazine*, CCXCVI (1904), 606-616. [317]

Deplores the fact that "to-day William Cowper is not read at all," contends that the centenary notices emphasized the man rather than the poet, and outlines reasons why Cowper should appeal to a wider range of readers.

Cecil, Lord David. "William Cowper," *Listener*, V (June 17, 1931), 1003-1005. [318]

The B.B.C. Third Program in commemoration of the bicentenary of the poet's birth. Contends that in Cowper's life and character, as in his works, "the strange contrasts . . . are, indeed, the most striking thing." Quotes "The Poplar-Field" and "On Receipt of My Mother's Picture."

Chapman, Edward M. "Dawn of a New Day," *English Literature in Account with Religion* (Boston: Houghton-Mifflin Company, 1910), 34-50. Also published as *English Literature and Religion* (London: Constable and Company, 1910). [319]

"[Cowper] became the accepted poet of the English Evangelicals, bringing sweetness and light into many middle-class homes where reawakened piety, threatening to degenerate into a new asceticism, needed him sorely enough."

Child, Harold. "William Cowper," *Cambridge History of English Literature*, edited by Ward and Waller (New York: Putnam, 1914), XI, 86-102. [320]

"Cowper, though not among the great poets of England, holds a unique place, partly by virtue of the personality which shines in every line of his poetry, partly . . . the sincerity and simplicity which . . . saw beauty in common things, till then neglected, but eagerly seized upon by his successors."

Clark, Henry W. "The Grown-Up Child in Cowper," *Contemporary Review*, CXXXIV (1928), 768-773.   [321]
  Cowper seen as "always simple, yet always looking far as we l as near."

Courthope, W. J. *A History of English Poetry* (London: Macmillan and Company, 1905), V, 113-116, 346-359.   [322]
  Emphasis on Cowper's religious lyricism.

Craig, Hardin, *et al.* *A History of English Literature* (New York: Oxford University Press, 1950), pp. 445-448.   [323]
  ". . . Cowper provided his many English admirers with a poetry that blended and harmonized Evangelical religion, the new sensibility, and democratic aspiration." [L. I. Bredvold.]

Davie, Donald. "The Critical Principles of William Cowper," *The Cambridge Journal*, VII (1953), 182-188.   [324]
  Cowper as a neo-classicist, "a defiant rearguard," rather than a pre-romanticist. Cf. 141.

———. *Purity of Diction in English Verse* (London: Chatto and Windus, 1952), pp. 51-61.   [325]
  Comments on Cowper's use of circumlocution in "The Castaway" ("a circumlocutory account of Cowper's damnation") and *The Task* ("one vast circumlocution . . . built out of repeated circumlocutions on a smaller scale").

Dewar, George A. B. "William Cowper," *Saturday Review*, LXXXIX (1900), 521.   [326]
  "[Cowper] loved nature as did Thomson, Gray, and other poets of the eighteenth century, fondly but complacently."

Dowden, Edward. *The French Revolution and English Literature* (New York: Charles Scribner's Sons, 1897), pp. 36-41.   [327]
  ". . . although he was far from being a spirit of Revolution, Cowper mourns in Revolutionary fashion over the growth of

luxury and the evils of a spurious civilization . . . He expresses no less clearly the humanitarian sentiment of the time." Cf. 258, 349.

Dykes, Eva Beatrice. *The Negro in English Romantic Thought* (Washington, D. C.: The Associated Publishers, 1942), pp. 15-18. [328]

Comments on Cowper's anti-slavery poetry. See Hartley (349), Klingberg (357), Sypher (402).

Dyson, H. V. D., and John Butt. *Augustans and Romantics, 1689-1830* (London: The Cresset Press [1940]), pp. 77-78, 189-190. [329]

Brief critical treatment with bibliography.—"It is easy to underrate Cowper, who made small claim for his own poetry. His satires are not now much read, but in the modest kingdom where he reigns he is a true king."

Elton, Oliver. *A Survey of English Literature, 1780-1830* (London: Edward Arnold, 1912), pp. 72-79. [330]

Cowper as the "renewer of poetical taste."

Emery, Clark Nixon. "Science and Eighteenth-Century Poetry," Seattle: University of Washington, 1940. (Unpublished doctoral dissertation.) [331]

Contains lengthy section on Cowper, for comments on which see Kroitor (358).

Enright, D. J. "Willian Cowper," *The Pelican Guide to English Literature, From Dryden to Johnson* (Harmondsworth, Middlesex: Penguin Books, Ltd., 1957), IV, 387-398. [332]

A compact and competent appraisal of Cowper's poetry and its place in the century.—"Cowper speaks with an individual, if quiet, voice, and . . . although he is unlikely to enjoy any future vogue, he has something to offer which will never fall entirely out of fashion or out of date."

Fairchild, Hoxie Neale. *The Noble Savage: A Study in Romantic Naturalism* (New York: Columbia University Press, 1928), pp. 70-75. [333]

"Cowper has so strong a Methodist strain that he cannot reconcile virtue with a life of tropical plenty." Cf. 407.

————. *Religious Trends in English Poetry*, II (New York: Columbia University Press, 1942), 171-190.   [334]

Religious elements in Cowper's life and works discussed, treating Cowper as "the one most important poet of the Evangelical Movement" whose "most important characteristic is his ability to subject to the purest Evangelicalism a nature-feeling much stronger and more genuine than that of most of his unorthodox sentimental contemporaries." Cf. 231, 278, 334, 359, 394.

Forster, Edward Morgan. "William Cowper, An Englishman," *Spectator*, CXLVIII (1932), 71.   [335]

Cowper is perishing from memory because England is perishing.—See reply by Sir Hugh Walpole, *ibid.*, p. 111, and the reply of R. B., p. 147.

Frazer, Sir James G. "William Cowper," *Sir Roger de Coverly and Other Literary Pieces* (London: Macmillan and Company, 1920).   [336]

Reprinted from *Nineteenth Century*, LXXXVII (1920), 1031-34. See the memoir introducing Frazer's edition of the *Letters* (121).

Garrod, H. W. "Books and Writers," *Spectator*, CLXXXVI (1951), 690.   [337]

"It has become the fashion to love [Cowper] for his letters and his loveableness, but to be lukewarm about his poetry."

Gill, Frederick C. *The Romantic Movement and Methodism* (London: The Epworth Press, 1937), pp. 129-147.   [338]

"Cowper found in Evangelicalism that warmth of both emotion and spiritual exaltation which set his own soul glowing, kindled his imagination, and prepared him for his greatest work .... The distinctive character of his religion is reflected in the integrity of his style." See Fairchild (334) and Lanham (359).

Glover, T. R. *Poets and Puritans* (London: Methuen, 1915), pp. 144-174.   [339]

A critical-biographical study with emphasis on the religious milieu.—"[Cowper's] letters and poems together give us such a picture as we have nowhere in English, save in Boswell and Lockhart—and one which, it is possible to say, surpasses both in charm."

Gosse, Sir Edmund. *English Literature: An Illustrated Record* (New York: Grosset and Dunlap, 1904), IV, 2-10.   [340]

> Cowper as an "extension" of Thomson, "advancing the exact observation of natural objects . . . without a trace of lyrical effusion . . . distinguished from his eighteenth-century predecessors by a resistance to their affected, rhetorical diction."

Grew, Eva Mary. "William Cowper and His Love of Music," *Chesterian*, XIII (June 1932), 185-187.   [341]

> See 705.

Grierson, Sir Herbert J. C., and J. C. Smith. *A Critical History of English Poetry* (New York: Oxford University Press, 1946), pp. 252-267.   [342]

> "Cowper, the man . . . is of greater interest today than his poems."

Griggs, Charles I. "Science in English Literature from Thomson to Cowper," *Summaries of Doctoral Dissertations, University of Wisconsin*, II (1938), 298-300.   [343]

> Contends that Cowper's use of science is slight and conventional and that his views are anti-rationalist and in marked contrast to those of Thomson and Aikenside. See Bush (315) and Kroiter (358).

Hamer, Enid. *The Metres of English Poetry* (London: Methuen, 1954), 111-113.   [344]

> Cowper comes at the end of the Miltonic tradition of blank verse.

Haney, J. L. *Early Reviews of English Poets* (Philadelphia: Edgerton Press, 1904), pp. 10-12.   [345]

> Reprints unfavorable review of the 1782 volume from the *Critical Review*.

Hannay, Neilson Campbell. "The Tragedy of Cowper," *SRL*, VIII
(November 28, 1931), 325-328.   [346]
   Cowper's suffering viewed as a means of artistic growth. An
essay on the bi-centenary of the poet's birth. Contains a hitherto
unpublished letter and an unpublished silhouette. See 231.

Hantsche, Arthur Max. *William Cowper, sein naturgefühl und seine
naturdichtung* (Dresden: Lehmannsche Buchdruckerei, 1901).
[Doctoral dissertation.]   [347]
   A study of Cowper's attitude toward nature, including consideration of his personal contact with nature, his objective
natural descriptions in his poetry, his subjective or lyric nature
poetry, and his poetic imagery drawn from nature. Concludes
that Cowper's *Naturgefühl* does much toward making him the
first modern English poet. See Huang (432) and Taffe (403); also
307.

Hartley, Lodwick. " 'The Stricken Deer' and His Contemporary
Reputation," *SP*, XXXVI (1939), 637-650.   [348]
   "[Contemporary] reviews leave little doubt that Cowper was
taken seriously both in his art and in his opinions."

———. *William Cowper, Humanitarian* (Chapel Hill: University of
North Carolina Press, 1938).   [349]
   Cowper's poetry as it reflects the humanitarian interests of the
century.—Reviewed in *TLS*, September 3, 1938, p. 565; Boston
Evening Transcript, June 9, 1938; *Books* of the New York *Herald-
Tribune*, August 28, 1938; Manchester *Guardian*, August 15, 1938;
TBR, December 25, 1938, p. 6; *Year's Work in English Studies*, IX
(1938), 280-281; *SRL*, June 18, 1938, p. 18; *Contemporary Review*,
CLIV (1938), 511; *American Historical Review*, XLIV (1939), 696-
697; *MLN*, LIV (1939), 391-392; *Catholic World*, CXLIX (1939),
374-375.—See 349, 402.

Hearn, Lafcadio. "Notes on Cowper," *Interpretations of Literature*,
edited by John Erskine, I (New York: Dodd, Mead and Company,
1924), 37-50.   [350]
   Lecture notes outlining reasons why Cowper can be read by
a modern reader, especially a Japanese. Emphasis on the poet's
skill in presenting realistic detail, on his "characters," and on his
satirical effectiveness.

Hoffman, [Carl] Willy. *William Cowpers belesenheit und literarische kritik* (Berlin: Mayer und Muller, 1908). [Doctoral dissertation.]   [351]

Chiefly a statistical study of books read and literary opinions expressed.—Reviewed *ES*, XLI (1910), 149-150.

Houtchens, Lawrence Huston, and Carolyn W. Houtchens, eds. *Leigh Hunt's Literary Criticism* (New York: Columbia University Press, 1956), pp. 138, 150, 393.   [352]

Hunt's opinions on Cowper's translations and poetry.—"He was alone, not because he led the way, but because he was left on the roadside." [p. 150]

Humphreys, A. R. *The Augustan World. Life and Letters in Eighteenth-Century England* (London: Methuen, 1945), *passim*.   [353]

Cowper's reflections on various aspects of eighteenth-century life: rural conditions, slavery, Calvinism, *et cetera*. See 349.

Irwin, Sidney T. "Satire and Poetry at Olney," *Independent Review*, VIII (1906), 293-305.   [354]

A review article discussing the editions of Cowper's poems by J. C. Bailey and H. S. Milford, both published in 1905. See 104, 130.

Jones, W. Powell. "The Captive Linnet: A Footnote on Eighteenth-Century Sentiment," *PQ*, XXXIII (1954), 330-337.   [355]

"William Cowper is the first of the eighteenth-century poets to register a definite protest against caged birds."

Ker, W. P. "William Cowper," *On Modern Literature* (Oxford: Clarendon Press, 1955), p. 231.   [356]

Lecture notes on Cowper's use of association of ideas, his blank verse, and his treatment of landscape.

Klingberg, Frank J. *The Anti-Slavery Movement in England* (New Haven: Yale University Press, 1926), pp. 67-70.   [357]

Cowper's influence in the anti-slavery movement.—See Dykes (328), Hartley (349), Sypher (402).

Kroitor, Harry Peter. "William Cowper and Science in the Eighteenth Century," *Dissertation Abstracts*, XVII (1957), 3018. (Abstract of a University of Maryland doctoral dissertation.) [358]

An examination of Cowper's interest in science as a key to neglected aspects of his work and as an approach to natural theology, deism, and didactic literature in the eighteenth century, placing the poet with the new apologetics at the end of the century in his championing of the God of Nature and the God of the Scriptures within a new scientific context. See Bush (315) and Griggs (343).

Lanham, Louise. "The Poetry of William Cowper in Its Relation to the English Evangelical Movement," *University of North Carolina Record: Research in Progress*, No. 311 (1936), pp. 44-45. (Abstract of a University of North Carolina doctoral dissertation.) [359]

A thoroughgoing study of the doctrinal background and implications of Cowper's poetry. Cf. Hannay (231) and Thein (278); also 334, 338, 394.

Law, Alice. "Cowper and Wordsworth," *Fortnightly Review*, LXXI (February 1902), 363-364. [360]

See also *Living Age*, CCXXXIII (1902), 316-318.—A reply to an article by Arthur Symons, "Wordsworth," *Living Age*, CCXXXII (1902), 796-806, characterizing Cowper's style as "mean."

———. "Some Beauties of Cowper," *Living Age*, CCIV (1895), 195-202. [361]

Lawton, Edith. "The Criticism of William Cowper," *Abstracts of Dissertations*, Boston University Graduate School, Boston, Massachusetts, 1941. (Abstract of a doctoral dissertation.) [362]

". . . his criticism like his poetry is that of a classical romanticist."

Legouis, Emile, and Louis Cazamian. *A History of English Literature* (New York: The Macmillan Company, 1929), pp. 958-962. [363]

"A great poet, though not one of the greatest . . . a foretaste of the coming renovation in literature." [Cazamian]

McCutcheon, Roger P. *Eighteenth-Century English Literature* (The Home University Library; New York: Oxford University Press, 1949), pp. 167-172. [364]

"Cowper's readers may find ample compensation in 'the harvest of the quiet eye' which he simply and yet richly spread throughout his pages."

McKillop, Alan Dugald. *English Literature from Dryden to Burns* (New York and London: Appleton-Century-Crofts, 1948), pp. 379-383. [365]

Chiefly factual. Brief bibliography.

MacLean, Kenneth. *Agrarian Age: A Background for Wordsworth* (New Haven: Yale University Press, 1950), pp. 34-36 [366]

Though Cowper had vision in world economy, he was almost totally blind "to the realities of the economy of his beloved scene."

———. "William Cowper," *The Age of Johnson: Studies Presented to Chauncey Brewster Tinker* (New Haven: Yale University Press, 1949), pp. 257-267. [367]

Contends that Cowper's poetry and letters appeal to the modern reader because they are "a record of a terror." "Neurosis and not the romantic movement was responsible for everything that he was as a writer." Cf. 120.

Manning, B. L. "History, Politics, and Religion in Certain Poems of William Cowper," *Congregational Quarterly*, VII (1929), 326-343. [368]

Cowper writes as "a Whig . . . peculiarly appreciative of our English parliamentary traditions, loyal to mild monarchy, rejoicing with a slightly superior air in that unique turn in our constitutional development which has saved us alone of all the world from the tyranny alike of monarchs and of revolutionaries; pious but utterly unclerical in point of view; critical of prelates and quietly scornful of those shallow persons who can see at a glance through the whole sham of the Christian religion . . . insular and rustic, but scholarly and gentle, a sort of etherealized and evangelized John Bull."

Monti, Giulio. "Nel secondo centenario della nascita di William Cowper," *Emporium* (Bergamo), LXXVI (1932), 339-355. [369]

An important essay considering Cowper's European reputation, surveying concisely his life and works, and attempting to place him in Western literature.—"L'ispirazione del Cowper, secondo lui [F. Philarète Chasles] è profondamente inglese . . . . Io direi piuttosta che l'ispirazione del Cowper, come quella dei grandi poeti dell'antichtià, è simplicemente *umana*, cioé di tutti i tempi e di tutti nazioni. Quel che fa vivere il Cowper è l'*umanità* che palpita e piange in tutta l'opera sua, quell'umanita che mancava ai poeti che lo han preceduto nel suo secolo." (The inspiration of Cowper according to him [Chasles] is profoundly English . . . . I would say rather that the inspiration of Cowper, like that of the great poets of antiquity, is simply *human*, that is of all times and all nations. What makes Cowper live is the *humanity* that pulses and weeps in all his work, that humanity which was lacking in the poets who came before him in his century.)

Moody, William Vaughan, and Robert Morss Lovett. *A History of English Literature* (New York: Charles Scribner's Sons, 1918), pp. 264-265. [370]

Typical perfunctory treatment of Cowper as a pre-romanticist,

Moulton, Charles Wells, *et al.* *The Library of Literary Criticism* (New York: Peter Smith, 1935), IV, 370-395. [371]

Excerpts from critical works; bibliography.

Neilson, William Allan. *Essentials of Poetry* (Boston: Houghton-Mifflin Company, 1912), pp. 142-143, 220-221. [372]

Comments on Cowper's realism and humanitarianism.

Nicholson, Norman. *William Cowper* (London: John Lehman. 1951). [373]

A comprehensive critical monograph. Reviewed by Edmund Blunden in *National and English Review*, CXXXVII (1951), 48-50; Patrick Dickson in *Fortnightly Review*, CLXX (1951), 640; *TLS*, June 29, 1952, p. 404; Lodwick Hartley in *PQ*, XXI (1951), 261-262; Edith J. Morley in *Year's Work in English Studies*, XXXII (1951), 211-212.

Olivero, Federico. "Un precursore del romanticismo inglese: William Cowper," *Nuova Antologia*, ser. 6, CCXXII [CCCVI] (January-February, 1923), 145-150.   [374]

  Presents Cowper as a forerunner of Wordsworth in his minutely accurate descriptions, his love of retirement and solitary meditation, and above all in his religious conception of the life and omnipresence of the Divinity in nature.—"Il Cowper prelude all'-Wordsworth col suo fedele minuto metodo di pittura, col suo amore di ritiro e di meditazione solinga sopratutto colla religiosa concezione della vita e dell-onnipresenza della Divinità nella natura."

Osgood, Charles Grosvenor. *The Voice of England* (New York: Harper and Brothers, 1935), pp. 373-379.   [375]
  "Cowper's is an art exquisitely pitched between the transcendent idyllism of Goldsmith and the literal reality of Crabbe."

Patrick, David, and J. Liddell Geddie, eds. "William Cowper," *Chambers's Cyclopaedia of English Literature* (Philadelphia and New York: J. B. Lippincott, 1938), II, 601-612.   [376]
  "[Cowper] was in the eighteenth century, but not of it. He manifestly stands at the parting of the ways, and did not fully embody, though he heralded the new spirit." (See also entries for John Newton and William Hayley, *ibid.*)

Possehl, Willi. *William Cowpers stellung zur religion* (Gr.-Lichterfelde: J. Unverdorben, 1907). [University of Rostock dissertation.]   [377]
  The pervasive influence of Pietism [*sic*] or Methodism on Cowper's concepts of God, Man, and Nature. See Hannay (231), Thein (278), and Lanham (359).

"Power and Gentleness," *TLS*, November 19, 1931, pp. 901-902. [378]
  A leading article based on Fausset's selection of the poems in Everyman's Library (120). Countering the editor's thesis that Cowper's poetry was "self defense," the article argues for the strength of the poet's utterance, calling him "a patriot of the metal of Milton and Marvell" with "a passion for integrity and nobility in national conduct," a writer whose poetry and letters are "actions, just and bright." Cf. 366.

Press, John. *The Fire and the Fountain* (London: Oxford University Press, 1955), pp. 6-11.   [379]

Cowper's madness in relation to his poetic inspiration.

Quayle, Thomas. *Poetic Diction: A Study of Eighteenth-Century Verse* (London: Methuen, 1924), pp. 48-50, 73-74, 168-173.   [380]

Though in his early work, Cowper uses "not a little of the language which he is at such pains to condemn," in *The Task*—especially in the parts involving natural description—the images are new and fresh and the language is, as a rule, simple. There is even more classical purity of poetic expression in the shorter poems and in the hymns.

Quiller-Couch, Sir Arthur. "Horatian Model in English Verse," *Studies in Literature* (New York: G. P. Putnam's Sons, 1926), I, 56, 68.   [381]

". . . of all our poets the one who, but for his stroke of madness, would have become our English Horace, was William Cowper." [p. 68]   See 707.

Quintus Quiz [Edward Shillito]. "I Sing the Sofa," *Christian Century*, LVIII (1941), 615-616.   [382]

"[Cowper] had the country-heart. Nonetheless, his poetry has the indefinable wit . . . of the cultivated and genteel in the salons of the city."

Ranger [pseud.] "William Cowper," *Bookman* (London), XXXI (1906), 22-24.   [383]

Cowper can best be described as "an essayist in verse." Cf. 404.

Richmond, W. Kenneth. *Poetry and the People* (London: Routledge, 1947), pp. 145-146.   [384]

"For Cowper . . . Nature . . . begins to show itself as a rudimentary philosophy, trite, no doubt—a philosophy that loses itself in floods of self-pity and soft sentiment, but nevertheless one which has become a part of him."

Rippey, Lydia Hulburt. "Cowper and the Critics," *University of Colorado Studies, Abstracts of Theses for Higher Degrees*, XX (1932-33), 83. (Abstract of a thesis for a Master's Degree.) [385]

The Task was sufficiently orthodox to appeal to the classicists and sufficiently different to please those who wished a change; but Cowper's reputation suffered when Wordsworth's was at its height. A Victorian revival of interest caused a gradual increase in popularity. A lively twentieth-century interest is noted. See Birrell (309).

Roy, James Alexander. *Cowper and His Poetry* (Poetry and Life Series; London: G. G. Harrap and Company, 1914). [386]

A thoroughgoing study of the poetry, though lacking in unusual critical perception. Contains bibliographical material of some value.

Saintsbury, George. *A History of English Prosody* (London: Macmillan and Company, 1908), II, 468-472, 495-499. [387]

Comments on Cowper's mastery of the couplet and blank verse. Cf. 314.

———. *The Peace of the Augustans* (London: G. Bell and Sons, 1916), 248-254, 331-342. [388]

"What Cowper might have been as a poet is perhaps only shown in *Yardley Oak* and *The Castaway*. The rest . . . is second-rate of various degrees . . . Cowper perhaps deserves the highest place among English letter writers."

———. *A Short History of English Literature* (London: Macmillan and Company, 1930), pp. 588-590. [389]

". . . we find in [Cowper] the oddest mixture of the old and new . . . his work contained the seeds, and showed the symptoms of impending revolution . . . Cowper's poetry inclines rather to the old than to the new."

Sampson, George. *The Concise Cambridge History of English Literature* (New York: The Macmillan Company, 1941), pp. 569-571. [390]

"William Cowper was a sweet, simple, instinctive poet, whom we should refuse to accept, at anybody's bidding, as the leader or forerunner, or anticipator of something called 'the romantic revolt.' "

Seccombe, Thomas. *The Age of Johnson* (London: G. Bell and Sons, 1899), pp. 259-273. [391]

Cowper as "the best of English letter writers and the most important poet in England between Pope . . . and Wordsworth." His verse marks "the commencement of political poetry in England . . . [he is] the first modern poet of fraternity, a harbinger in a measure of Burns, of Whitman, and of Tolstoi."

Shafer, Robert. "William Cowper. Born 26 November 1731," *AB*, LXXIV (1931-32), 287-297. [392]

Among the best of the bi-centenary appreciations.—"[Cowper's] is silver verse, not golden . . . Yet something he had which endeared him to those who knew him when he lived . . . and which continues to make him a poet who is loved while other greater men may be truly but more distantly admired . . . [in] *The Task* . . . Cowper transmuted much good sense into true poetry."

Sharp, Robert Farquharson. "Cowper the Man," *Architects of Literature* (New York: E. P. Dutton and Company, 1900), 121-122. [393]

Essentially a critical-biographical appreciation.—"The quiet elegance of *The Task*, the fun of *John Gilpin*, the easy wit of Cowper's letters, are not what one would expect from a diseased mind."

Shepherd, T. B. *Methodism and the Literature of the Eighteenth Century* (London: The Epworth Press, 1940), 239-243. [394]

". . . while it must be admitted that, in his periods of insanity, Cowper's Calvinism intensified his depression and suffering, any fair account of Cowper must also show that his whole life and being was saturated with Evangelical religion." See Lanham (359).

Shorter, Clement K. "To the Immortal Memory of William Cowper," *Immortal Memories* (New York and London: Harper and Brothers, 1907), pp. 31-57. [395]

Originally an address entitled "The Sanity of Cowper" for the celebration of the centenary of Cowper's death at Olney, August

25, 1900.—The poet's humor is emphasized as the essential note of his sanity.

Sidgwick, Arthur. "Cowper," *Saint George*, V (1902), 116-132.   [396]

"Some English Views of Cowper," *Literary Digest*, XX (June 2, 1900), 661-662.   [397]
  Sums up centenary appraisals of Cowper, quoting Birrell (309), Dewar (326), and Spender (398).

Spender, A. Edward. "The Centenary of Cowper," *Westminster Review*, CLIII (1900), 532-545.   [398]
  "First of poets, since the days of Milton, to champion the sacredness of religion, he was the forerunner of a new school that disliked the political satires of the disciples of Pope, and aimed at borrowing for their lines of song from the simple beauties of a perfect nature."

Steele, F. M. "Catholicism and English Literature in the Eighteenth Century," *American Catholic Quarterly*, XXXVI (1911), 634-649.   [399]
  Comments on Cowper's relationship with the Throckmortons. See 204.

Stephen, Sir Leslie. *English Literature and Society in the Eighteenth Century* (New York and London: G. P. Putnam's Sons, 1907), pp. 204-208.   [400]
  Cowper's "sentimentalism" and "return to nature" compared with Goldsmith's, Rousseau's, and Crabbe's.

Sutherland, James. *A Preface to Eighteenth Century Poetry* (Oxford: Clarendon Press, 1948), *passim*.   [401]
  Contains important comments on Cowper's place in eighteenth-century poetry.

Sypher, Wylie. *Guinea's Captive Kings: British Anti-Slavery Literature of the Eighteenth Century* (Chapel Hill: University of North Carolina Press, 1942), pp. 186-189.   [402]
  Minimizes the importance of Cowper's anti-slavery verse. Cf. Dykes (328), Hartley (349), Klingberg (357).

Taffe, Valentine. "Le sentiment de la nature chez Cowper," *Revue Anglo-Américaine*, IV (1927), 308-319.   [403]

A study of the nature poetry with emphasis on the freshness and accuracy of the natural description, together with attention to the origin of the poet's attitude toward nature in his religious beliefs.—"Artiste, poète, croyant, telles sont les trois attitudes de Cowper en présence de la nature . . . ." See Hantsche (347) and Huang (432).

Thomas, Gilbert. "William Cowper," *Contemporary Review*, CXL (1911), 621-628.   [404]

"If Lamb be the poet among our essayists, Cowper is certainly the Elia among our poets."   Cf. 383.

Thompson, Harold William, ed. *The Anecdotes and Egotisms of Henry Mackenzie*, 1745-1831 (London: Oxford University Press, 1927), pp. 165-166.   [405]

Mackenzie's comments on Cowper's natural style ("frequently prosaic and what I would call *husky* . . . somewhat like Donne modernized") and his "good sense," with a comparison of the poet with Collins. See 442.

Thomson, J. A. K. *The Classical Background of English Literature* (London: George Allen and Unwin, 1948), pp. 209-210.   [406]

"In Cowper we see the fading of the classical impulse."

Tinker, Chauncey B. *Nature's Simple Plan* (Princeton: Princeton University Press, 1922), pp. 86-88.   [407]

Comments on Cowper's position on primitivism. See Fairchild (333).

Traill, H. D., ed. *Social England* (New York: G. P. Putnam's Sons, 1896), V, 442-444.   [408]

Special praise for *Table Talk* as "admirably just and searching criticism . . . a performance of extraordinary merit." Sees "essential conservatism" in *The Task*, but praises the unmistakable accent of truth in passages of natural description.

Turner, W. J., ed. *The Romance of English Literature* (New York: Hastings House, 1941), 49-51, 76-77. [409]

Sir Herbert Grierson comments briefly on the hymns and Lord David Cecil on the source of Cowper's inspiration.

Vaughan, Charles Edwyn. *The Romantic Revolt* (New York: Charles Scribner's Sons, 1907), pp. 16-27. [410]

Cowper "stands . . . at the parting of the ways: half disciple of the old order, half, indeed more than half, a standard-bearer of the new."

Vines, Sherard. *The Course of English Classicism* (New York: Harcourt, Brace and Company, 1930), pp. 133-134. [411]

". . . in Cowper . . . there still lingers something of the strength and majesty that classic schooling alone can impart; Cowper's handling of the couplet reflects the twilight of this nobility."

Warren, C. H. "Revaluations," *Outlook* (London), LXI (1928), 813-814. [412]

Contends that "Mrs. Unwin, Lady Austen, Lady Hesketh, and, most blameable of all, the Rev. John Newton . . . muddied the clear well of [Cowper's] genius," that the letters contain more poetry than his verse, and that when Cowper freed himself from his limiting circumstances he was a poet "in advance of his time."

Waugh, Arthur. "William Cowper," *Fortnightly Review*, CXXXVI (1931), 590-603. [413]

A bi-centenary essay of genuine merit.—"He looked into his heart and wrote, and against that sort of witness time and change are powerless . . . Our present understanding of him is perhaps the most shining example of the antiseptic grace of human sincerity. And in that saving quality he was a pioneer in his own generation."

Wood, Frederick T. "William Cowper: A Bi-Centenary Study," *Poetry Review* XXII (1931), 409-423. [414]

A sentimentalized appreciation based chiefly on Cecil's biography.

Woodberry, George Edward. "Three Men of Piety," *Makers of Literature* (New York: The Macmillan Company, 1907), pp. 271-301. [415]

An essay on Bunyan, Cowper, and Channing.

Young, Sir George. *An English Prosody on Inductive Lines* (Cambridge: Cambridge University Press, 1928), p. 111. [416]

"Cowper's verse, in *The Task* and *Yardley Oak*, has nerve; his lines are not padded with adjectives; they swing, if they cannot roll and break, though they never soar."

B. LITERARY RELATIONS AND INFLUENCES

Batdorf, Franklin P. "The Background of Crabbe's 'Village,' " *N&Q*, CXCIV (1949), 477-478. [425]

Suggests influence of Cowper.

Beach, Joseph Warren. *The Concept of Nature in Nineteenth-Century English Poetry* (New York: The Macmillan Company, 1936), pp. 37-49. [426]

Cowper's nature concepts compared with Wordsworth's. See 439.

Coburn, Kathleen, ed. *The Notebooks of Samuel Taylor Coleridge.* 2 vols. (London: Routledge and Kegan Paul; New York: Pantheon Books, Inc., 1957), *passim*. [427]

Consult index for Coleridge's general references to Cowper and quotations from his poems. See also Morley (712).

Ferguson, J. Delancey, ed. *Letters of Robert Burns* (Oxford: Oxford University Press, 1931), I, 260; II, 225. [428]

Burns's praise of Cowper.

Ford, C. Lawrence. "Cowper and Voltaire," *N&Q*, 10th ser., IV (December 9, 1905), 465. [429]

A possible indebtedness to Voltaire.

Havens, Raymond Dexter. *The Influence of Milton on English Poetry* (Cambridge, Massachusetts: Harvard University Press, 1922), pp. 161-176. [430]

Though Milton's influence was pervasive, it was (except perhaps in the Cowper's Homeric translations) a matter of assimilation rather than servile imitation.

Holmes, E. D. "The Question of Cowper's Indebtedness to Churchill," *MLN*, XIII (1898), 330-339. [431]

Contends that Cowper's indebtedness to Churchill has been greatly exaggerated.

Howard, Leon. *The Connecticut Wits* (Chicago: The University of Chicago Press, 1943), *passim*. [431a]

Consult index for references to the relationship of Cowper to the Connecticut Wits, particularly Timothy Dwight.

Huang, Roderick. *William Cowper: Nature Poet* (Oxford: Oxford University Press for the University of Malaya, 1957). [432]

Cowper's relation to the Georgic tradition of didactic-descriptive poetry in the eighteenth century and the influence of Methodism—particularly through James Hervey—on the nature poetry. See Hantsche (347) and Taffe (403); also 307, 718.

Keynes, Geoffrey, ed. *The Letters of William Blake* (London: Rupert Hart-Davis, 1956), pp. 81-88, 115-117. [433]

Blake's part in Cowper's *Milton*, in Hayley's *Life*, and in the design for Cowper's monument. See Bentley (202) and Ryskamp (1022).

Langston, C. J. "William Cowper and Edward Gibbon: A Contrast," *Argosy* (London), LXVI (1898), 124-128. [434]

Women and religion in the lives of two very different eighteenth-century writers. A *tour de force* with more purple prose than substance.

Mabbott, Thomas Olive. "Keats and Cowper: A Reminiscence?" *N&Q*, CLXXV (September 3, 1938), 170. [435]

Possible indebtedness of Keat's sonnet "When I have fears" to Cowper's "Stanzas subjoined to the yearly bill of mortality . . . for the year 1788."

Martin, L. C. "Vaughan and Cowper," *MLR*, XXII (1927), 79-
84.   [436]
　　Suggests possibility that reading of Vaughan may have had
some part in changing Cowper's attitude toward external nature.

Nethercot, Arthur H. "The Reputation of the 'Metaphysical Poets,' "
SP, XXII (1925), 107-108.   [437]
　　Cowper's interest in Cowley, Herbert, and Donne. See 709.

Norman, Herbert J. *Cowper and Blake* (Olney: The Cowper Society,
1913).   [438]
　　The relationship of the two poets in Cowper's last years
through the common friendship of William Hayley. See Bishop
(203); also 202, 211, 222.

Parrington, Vernon L. *Main Currents in American Thought: The
Romantic Revolution in America* (New York: Harcourt Brace and
Company, 1927), II, 88.   [439]
　　Notes the influence of Cowper on the verse of young Phila-
delphians *circa* 1800.

Potts, Abbie Findlay. *Wordsworth's "Prelude": A Study of Its
Literary Form* (Ithaca, New York: Cornell University Press, 1953),
pp. 350-357.   [440]
　　The influence of Cowper on Wordsworth. See also Morley
(712).

Thomas, Walter. *Le Poète Edward Young* (Paris: Hachette et cie.,
1901), pp. 494-495.   [441]
　　The influence of Young on Cowper.

Thompson, Harold William. *A Scottish Man of Feeling* (London and
New York: Oxford University Press, 1931), pp. 329-331.   [442]
　　The epistolary friendship of Cowper and Henry Mackenzie.
See 405.

Tietje, Gustav. *Die poetische personifikation unpersonliche sub-
stantiva bei Cowper und Coleridge* (Kiel: C. H. Jebens, 1914).
[Doctoral dissertation.]   [443]

Tillotson, Geoffrey. "Matthew Arnold and Eighteenth Century Poetry," *Essays on the Eighteenth Century Presented to David Nichol Smith* (Oxford: Clarendon Press, 1945), pp. 263-265.   [444]

    Arnold's comments on the Miltonic influence on Cowper.

Wright, H. G. "The Relations of the Welsh Bard Iolo Morganwy with Dr. Johnson, Cowper, and Southey," *RES*, VIII (1932), 129-138.   [445]

    Concerns Cowper's meeting the Welsh bard in London in the autumn of 1792 through the good offices of Samuel Rose.

Yardley, E. "Cowper [as a Parodist]," *N&Q*, 9th ser., V (January 20, 1900), 44-45, 96.   [446]

    Notes on Cowper's parody of Milton; also the influences of Thomson, Philips, and Somervile on the poet.

C. THE OLNEY HYMNS

Bailey, Albert Edward. *The Gospel in Hymns, Backgrounds and Interpretations* (New York: Charles Scribner's Sons, 1950), pp. 131-135.   [500]

    Interpretations of "God moves in a mysterious way," "Oh! for a closer walk," and "Sometimes a light surprises."

Bayne, Thomas. "Isaac Watts and Cowper," *N&Q*, 10th ser., II (October 22, 1904), 323.   [501]

    Similarity of fourth stanza of Watts's "Heavenly Joy on Earth" to opening stanza of Cowper's "Light Shining Out of Darkness."

Benson, Louis F. *The English Hymn* (New York: George H. Doran Company, 1915), pp. 336-340.   [502]

    Regards *Olney Hymns* as bringing Evangelical hymnody to a close: "the offices of the Prayer Book yield to the sermon, the church year is superseded by the civil, the sacraments are subordinated, and the Revival method expresses itself in evangelical theology, the strenuous activity in the sphere of individual emotion, the didactic element . . . and the expository dealings with the Scriptures."

———. *The Hymnody of the Christian Church* (New York: George H. Doran, [1927], p. 123. [503]

"It was the singular vitality of Newton's contributions rather than the delicacy of Cowper's that made their *Olney Hymns* a classic manual of Evangelical discipline."

———. *Studies of Familiar Hymns, Second Series* (Philadelphia: The Westminster Press, 1923), pp. 142-151. [504]

The background of "God moves in a mysterious way."

Fox, Adam. *English Hymns and Hymn Writers* (Britain in Pictures Series; London: Collins, 1947). [505]

Includes a brief appreciation of Cowper as a hymn writer and his place in English hymnody.

Gillman, Frederick John. *The Evolution of the English Hymn* (London: George Allen and Unwin, [1927]), pp. 232-238. [506]

Recognizes the lyrical and autobiographical quality of Cowper's hymns.—"Their self-conscious and overwrought fervour makes them, as a rule, unfit for congregational singing."

Gregory, Arthur E. *The Hymn-Book of the Modern Church* (London: Charles H. Kelly, 1904), pp. 233-234. [507]

". . . the Olney Hymns, even at their feeblest, have life and vigour, and are often provokingly easy to remember. Their influence on modern hymnody has been all in favour of the expression of personal, individual experience, in which regard they may not unfairly be compared with many of the sublimest psalms."

Hartley, Lodwick. "The Worm and the Thorn: A Study of Cowper's *Olney Hymns*," *Journal of Religion*, XXIX (1949), 220-229. [508]

Argues for more subjective elements in the hymns than Fairchild (334), Keck (510), and others are willing to allow.

Johansen, John Henry. *The Olney Hymns, The Papers of the Hymn Society*, XX (New York: The Hymn Society of America, 1956). [509]

A pamphlet containing a compendium of critical opinion, second-hand biographical material, and a useful bibliography. Stresses the facts that the Olney hymnbook was intended for midweek evangelical meetings rather than for church services, that "the unbounded love of the Savior" is Newton's principal note, and that Cowper's hymns in general have greater depth and tenderness than Newton's.

Keck, Wendell M. "Cowper's *Olney Hymns:* A Theological Study," *Abstracts of Dissertations,* Stanford University, 1940-41, pp. 87-89. (Doctoral dissertation.) [510]

A thorough going study of the doctrinal background of the hymns.—"The experiential hymns have a testimonial rather than expository tone . . . the personal tone of these testimonials is to be taken as conventional expression, not as Cowperian autobiography." Cf. Hartley (508).

Knight, George Litch. "William Cowper as a Hymn Writer," *The Hymn,* I (1950), 5-12, 20. [511]

A summary of critical opinions and an assessment of the contemporary popularity of the hymns, quoting extensively from Hartley (508).

Lynn, W. T. "Cowper's 'God Moves in a Mysterious Way,'" *N&Q,* 11th ser., III (January 21, 1911), 58. [512]

Answering Watson Surr's query in *ibid.,* p. 10, regarding correct reading of the hymn. See also *ibid.,* p. 153 (February 25, 1911), Bailey (500), and Benson (502).

Macmillan, Alexander. *Hymns of the Church* (Toronto: The United Church Publishing House, [1945]), pp. 154-161. [513]

A general discussion of the *Olney Hymns,* with emphasis on the lyrical quality of Cowper's contributions.

Manuscripts of the Earl of Dartmouth. Historical Manuscripts Commission, 15th Report, III (London, 1896), Appendix, Part 1, 245, 248. [514]

Three letters from Newton to Lord Dartmouth concerning the *Olney Hymns.*

Marks, Harvey Blair. *The Rise and Growth of English Hymnody* (New York: Fleming H. Revell, [1938]), pp. 109-114. [515]

A routine and unilluminating comparison of hymns by Newton and Cowper.

Moffatt, James, and Millar Patrick. *Handbook to the Church Hymnary.* (London: Oxford University Press [1935?]), pp. 13, 72, 88, 141, 150-151, 156-157, 234-235, 308-309.   [516]

Brief biographical sketch with general critical estimate of the hymns. Valuable notes on several hymns, especially "Oh! for a closer walk" and "There is a fountain."—"In his hymns [Cowper] is scarcely seen at his best, though some of them are touchingly beautiful."

Pollard, Arthur F. "William Cowper's Olney Hymns: A Critical Study," *The Churchman* (London), LXIX, No. 3 (July-September, 1955), pp. 166-171.   [517]

General critical evaluation; especially interesting for a defence of the controversial "There is a fountain": "Its doctrine is impeccable, its mood passionately sincere, its statement simple and direct, and it presents an experience which, though necessarily in varying measure, ought to be shared with Cowper by all his Christian readers." See Johansen (509).

Quinlan, Maurice J. "Cowper's [Biblical] Imagery," *JEGP*, XLVII (1948), 276-285.   [518]

Argues that the recurrence of certain imagery bore a special relationship to Cowper's fears and melancholy obsessions. (Most of this material is included in Quinlan's *William Cowper*, and the treatment of the imagery is expanded. See 257.)

Reeves, Jeremiah Bascomb. *The Hymn in History and Literature* (New York and London: The Century Company, 1924) [Also issued as *The Hymn as Literature*], pp. 201-204.   [519]

Routley, Erik. *Hymns and Human Life* (London: John Murray, [1952]), pp. 75-78.   [520]

Contrasts hymns of Newton and Cowper.—"[Cowper's] hymns are hymns of passionate Christian experience, the hymns of the introvert . . . . Newton at his best was always a writer for the church, while Cowper excelled in the hymn of personal devotion."

For additional material on the hymns, see 273, 334, 409.

D. John Gilpin

Breslar, M. L. R. "John Gilpin's Route," *N&Q*, 9th ser., XII
(November 28, 1903), 437. [600]

Apropos of John Gilpin's carrying wine, this article discusses
customs governing wine in commercial rooms of country hotels of
the period.—"In those days any proposition to provide one's own
wine would have been looked upon as a mark of lunacy in the
proposer."

Butterworth, S. "Cowper, Lamb, or Hood?" *N&Q*, 10th ser., VII
(January 5, 1907), 11. [601]

A reply to query by "D. M." (10th ser., VI, 490) concerning
stanzas on Mrs. John Gilpin ascribing these stanzas to Charles
Lamb.

Carver, P. L. "A Continuation of John Gilpin," *RES*, VIII (1932),
205-210. [602]

A continuation by Henry Lemoine.

Coleman, A. M. "Illustrated Editions of John Gilpin," *N&Q*,
CLXVIII (February 2, 1935), 86. [603]

Notes "about a dozen" illustrated editions between 1828
[Cruikshank's illustrations] and 1911. See 612.

Collins, A. S. *The Profession of Letters* (London: Routledge and Sons,
1928), pp. 81-82, 91-92, 106-107. [604]

References to the circumstances of publication of Cowper's
works, especially "John Gilpin" and the *Homer*.

F., J. T. "John Gilpin's Route," *N&Q*, 9th ser., XII (September 12,
1903), 217. [605]

Gilpin left Cheapside at the West End, riding through St.
Martin's-le-Grand, Aldersgate Street, Goswell Street, Goswell
Road, bearing to the right through Islington, *et cetera*. See 607,
608, 615.

Förster, Max. "Cowpers Ballade 'John Gilpin.' Textgestalt, Ver-
breitung und Fortsetzungen," *ES*, LXIV (1929), 380-417; LXV
(1930-31), 26-48. [606]

An important comprehensive study of the text, the dissemination, and the translations, including a critical text of the poem.

See comments in *N&Q*, CLVIII (January 25, 1930), 56; and Wells (621).

Fry, Lucius G. "John Gilpin," *Cowper in London, Papers Read Before the Cowper Society* (London: Everett, 1907). [607]
Identifies John Gilpin as John Beyer (see 609, 610); attempts to determine Gilpin's route from the top of Cheapside to Edmonton (see 605, 608); corrects two "slight" topographical errors; describes the "Bell."

———. "John Gilpin's Route," *N&Q*, 9th ser., XII (September 26, 1903), 255. [608]
See above.

Harland-Oxley, W. E. "The Cowper Centenary," *N&Q*, 9th ser., V (May 5, 1900), 357-358. [609]
A reply to a query of John C. Francis, *ibid.*, pp. 301-309; chiefly concerning "John Gilpin." Argues that the hero's name could not have come from the tomb of John Gilpin in St. Margaret's Churchyard, Westminster.—See 611.

Humphreys, A. L. "Horsemen on the Great North Road," *N&Q*, CLXXX (June 21, 1941), 434-436. [610]
Discusses John Beyer as the original of John Gilpin. See 607.

Jonas, Alfred Charles. "Cowper's John Gilpin," *N&Q*, 10th ser. VII (May 25, 1907), 407-408; see also *ibid.*, p. 516 (June 29, 1907). [611]
Identifies John Gilpin of Croyden "or one of his family" as the probable hero of Cowper's poem. See 609.

Kirby, H. T. "John Gilpin in Picture: Some Illustrators of Cowper's Famous Poem," *Bookman*, LXXXI (1931), 198-200. [612]
An account of the way in which John Gilpin has been presented by illustrators from the crude chap-book artists through Cruikshank, Fitz-Cook, and Seccombe to Caldecott ("the greatest illustrator of Cowper's poems") and Brock. See 115, 116, 117, 603.

———. "John Gilpin," *Print Collector's Quarterly*, XXIII (July 1936), 167-186. [613]
The illustrated editions of "John Gilpin." See 612 above.

L., F. deH. "John Gilpin in Latin Elegiacs," *N&Q*, 11th ser., IX
(June 27, 1914), 513.   [614]

Reference to Latin translation in pamphlet by J. Vincent of
Oxford published in 1841.

Lucas, E. V. *A Wanderer in London* (London: Macmillan and Company, 1906), 145-150.   [615]

On the route of John Gilpin. See 605, 607, 608.

Page, John T. "John Gilpin's Route," *N&Q*, 9th ser., XII (November 7, 1903), p. 371.   [616]

Note on John Beyer's shop in Cheapside. Disputes Fry's idea
(607) that the name of the hero came from the tomb of a John
Gilpin buried in St. Margaret's Churchyard, Westminster. See
also Harland-Oxley (609).

Rae, Fraser. "John Gilpin: Shakespeare in 1790," *N&Q*, 9th ser.,
XII (July 11, 1903), 26.   [617]

Counters the idea that John Gilpin was "one John Beyer, who
lived in Cheapside and died in Bath in 1790" by a search of the
Bath Chronicle for 1790 which lists nobody by the name of Beyer.
Cf. Jonas (611), Humphreys (610), and Wake (618).

Wake, Joan. "John Gilpin," *TLS*, April 11, 1942, p. 192.   [618]

Suggests John Gilpin of Walton Hall in North Bucks as a
possible original of Cowper's hero. See Jonas (611), Humphreys
(610), Rae (617).

Ward, A. C. *Illustrated History of English Literature* (London:
Longmans, Green and Company, 1955), III, 20-23.   [619]

Contains facsimile of "John Gilpin" as a broadside ballad.

Weiss, Harry B. "William Cowper's Frolic in Rhyme: The Diverting
History of John Gilpin," *Bulletin of the New York Public Library*,
XLI (1937), 675-680.   [620]

Chiefly bibliographical. See 603 and 612.

Wells, John Edwin. "John Gilpin and Charles Lamb," *ES*, LXVII
(1932-33), 318-319.   [621]

Corrects Förster (606) on one of the sequels.

E. The Task

Craven, Dorothy H. "Cowper's Use of 'Slight Connection' in *The Task*: a Study of Structure and Style," *University of Colorado Studies*, Gen. Ser., XXIX, iii (1954), 4-6. (Abstract of a doctoral dissertation.)   [700]
  The use of "slight connection" and the "associational technique," in relation to Cowper's accomplishment in blank verse.

Deane, C. V. *Aspects of Eighteenth-Century Nature Poetry* (Oxford: Basil Blackwell, 1935), pp. 95-99.   [701]
  Cowper's use of the principles of visual composition in *The Task* as compared with Thomson's use of the same principles in *The Seasons.*—"In Thomson the strokes, the grouping of masses is bolder and simpler . . . while Cowper's style is more akin to that of Crome or Constable."

De Selincourt, Ernest, ed. *The Letters of William and Dorothy Wordsworth: The Latter Years* (Oxford: Clarendon Press, 1939), III, 1063-1064.   [702]
  Wordsworth on Cowper's indebtedness to Shenstone and Horace in *The Task*, IV.

Durling, Dwight. *Georgic Tradition in English Poetry* (New York: Columbia University Press, 1935), pp. 152-157.   [703]
  Cowper's major work placed in the didactic-descriptive tradition.—"*The Task* stimulated descriptive poetry, afforded new models, encouraged a less turgid, more natural style in blank verse, and gave new impetus to the search for exactitude and truth."

Fox, Robert C. "William Cowper and the Submarine," *N&Q*, CCII (1957), 360.   [704]
  Queries reference to "submarine exploits" in *The Task*, IV, 85.

Grew, Sydney and Eva Mary. "William Cowper: His Acceptance and Rejection of Music," *Music and Letters*, XIII (1932), 31-41.   [705]
  Concerns Cowper's strictures on the Handel Festival of 1784 in *The Task*, VI, and other references to music. See 341 and 713.

Humphreys, A. L. "Cowper on Langford" [*The Task*, VI, 287],
   N&Q, 11th ser., IV (August 19, 1911), 151.   [706]
   Note on "the Langford of the show," famous auctioneer. See
   also *ibid.* (September 9, 1911), p. 215.

Johnston, Mary. "Horace, Pliny the Younger, and Cowper," *Classi-*
   cal Weekly, XXVII (1933), 45-46.   [707]
   The Task, I, 242-248, as a modern commentary on the Roman
   fondness for shaded walks as described in Horace and Pliny the
   Younger. See 381.

Ker, W. P. *Form and Style in Poetry*, edited by R. W. Chambers
   (London: Macmillan and Company, 1928), pp. 170-171.   [708]
   Comments on Cowper's diction, particularly in *The Task.*—
   "Cowper had an extraordinary variety of language . . . [it] is of
   the purest and finest, but it is not strikingly ornamental."

Legouis, Pierre. "John Donne and William Cowper (A Note on *The*
   Task, III, 712-724)," *Anglia*, LXXVI (1958), 536-538.   [709]
   An inconclusive argument for the influence of Donne, with an
   observation on the contrast in the meaning of "nature" in the two
   poets. See 437.

M[abbott], T[homas] O. "A [Garden] Reference in Cowper," *N&Q*,
   CLXXXI (1941), 293.   [710]
   Reference in *The Task*, III, 642-647, to a garden design rep-
   resenting a zodiac, made up of pebbles or larger stones. See *N&Q*,
   CLXXXI (1941), 146.

Miles, Josephine. *Eras and Modes in English Poetry* (Berkeley and
   Los Angeles: University of California Press, 1957), pp. 114-
   115.   [711]
   The relation of *The Task* to the "Romantic Mode."

Morley, Edith. *Henry Crabb Robinson on Books and Their Writers*
   (London: J. M. Dent [1938]), I, 72, and *passim*.   [712]
   The indefatigable diarist's comments on the popularity of *The*
   Task and his statement that Johnson, the publisher, made
   £10,000 from Cowper's works [p. 72]. See index for general
   critical comments on the poet.

Myers, Robert Manson. "Fifty Sermons on Handel's Messiah," *Harvard Theological Review*, XXXIX (1946), 217-241. [713]

John Newton's sermon on the *Messiah* and Cowper's strictures on the Handel Festival of 1784 in *The Task*, VI. See Grew (705).

O'Brien, Justin. "La mémoire involuntaire avant Marcel Proust," *Revue de littérature comparée*, XIX (1939), 19-36. [714]

Comments on *The Task*, I, 1-18, as an example of pre-Proustian involuntary memory.

Patton, Julia. *The English Village: A Literary Study*, 1750-1850 (New York: The Macmillan Company, 1919), pp. 107-112. [715]

In *The Task* Cowper presents varied and familiar aspects of village life "in glimpses or in detailed description, faithfully and sympathetically."

Pierce, Frederick E. *Currents and Eddies in the English Romantic Generation* (New Haven: Yale University Press, 1918), pp. 19-32. [716]

Pertinent comments on the background of the popularity of *The Task*.

Price, Warwick James. "Cowper's *Task*: A Literary Milestone," *SR*, XXIV (1916), 155-164. [717]

Deplores the neglect of Cowper, arguing that he, "not Burns . . . is the real bridge between Thomson and Wordsworth."

Reynolds, Myra. *The Treatment of Nature in English Poetry* (Chicago: University of Chicago Press, 1907), pp. 184-194. [718]

The Task in relation to the new attitude toward nature. See 307, 347, 403, 432.

Stauffer, Donald A. *The Nature of Poetry* (New York: W. W. Norton and Company, 1946), p. 61. [719]

"Cowper's *The Task* is well named for the long stretches that present rural and domestic life in all its minute fragments: fewer parts would have made a greater whole."

Wormhoudt, Arthur. "Cowper's *The Task*, IV, 36-41," *Explicator*, VII (1948), item 4. [720]

    Points out the occurrence of the phrase "cheer but not inebriate" in Bishop Berkeley's *Siris* as a reference to tar water and suggests that Cowper's famous passage may have reference to that beverage rather than to tea.

F. Minor Poems and Translations

Battenham, E. N. "An Epigram," *TLS*, June 1, 1933, p. 380. [800]

    Johnson's epigram on Molly Aston as the source of Cowper's translated "Epigram" in *New Poems* (1931).

Bayne, Thomas. "Cowper's 'Charity' [1. 459]: 'Porcelain,' " *N&Q*, 11th ser., III (June 10, 1911), 409, 456, 498. [801]

    Cowper's reference explained by the assumption that porcelain articles were probably very expensive in the poet's day; hence the poet regarded porcelain as a symbol of self-indulgence.

Carmichael, Montgomery. "Cowper's Selkirk," *TLS*, July 30, 1931, p. 597. [802]

    Cites omission of the fourth stanza (containing "churchgoing bell") in various anthologies—Palgrave, Lang, Peacock, and especially *Beauties of English Poetry* (Paris, 1803), edited by Vergani—as well as omissions of stanzas in the earliest versions of the poem.

Doughty, Oswald. *Forgotten Lyrics of the Eighteenth Century* (London: H. F. and G. Witherby, 1924), pp. 19-21, and *passim*. [803]

    Reprints Cowper's reply to Mrs. Greville's "Prayer for Indifference" and comments on Cowper's lyricism in general.

Gilbert, Dorothy Lloyd, and Russell Pope. "The Cowper Translation of Mme. Guyon's Poems," *PMLA*, LIV (1939), 1077-1098. [804]

    Points out the "minor critique" growing up around Cowper's translation and reflecting the attempt of interpretive criticism to relate the poet's obsession of damnation to his religious creed. Argues that Cowper omitted the extreme passivity and the religious eroticism of the original. See Hartley (807).

Harting, J. E., *et al.* "Cowper's Nightingale," *N&Q*, CXLVIII (April 4, 1925), 245; and (April 18, 1925), 282-283.   [805]

A conjecture that Cowper might have mistaken the bird in "To a Nightingale" for a thrush, together with a discussion of the first publication of the poem and the circumstance that occasioned the poem as recorded in Cowper's letter to John Johnson on March 11, 1792.

Hartley, Lodwick. "Cowper and the Polygamus Parson," *MLQ*, XVI (1955), 137-141.   [806]

Demonstrates that the controversy over the publication of *Thelyphthora* by Cowper's cousin, the Reverend Martin Madan, and Cowper's attempt at satire in *Anti-Thelyphthora* stimulated the poet to embark on a major literary undertaking. See Lanham (359).

————. "Cowper and Mme. Guyon: Additional Notes," *PMLA*, LVI (1941), 585-587.   [807]

Shows how conclusions arrived at by Dorothy L. Gilbert and Russell Pope (804) had been anticipated by an anonymous biographer in 1803.

————. "Cowper's *The Castaway*," *Explicator*, V (1946), item 21.   [808]

Concerns the interpretation of the second stanza of the poem.

Hartmann, Hermann. "Über William Cowpers Tirocinium," *Festschrift zum Siebzigsten Geburtstage Oskar Schades dargebract von seinen Schüler und Verehren* (Königsberg, 1896), pp. 375-397. [809]

A study based on inadequate sources and a slight understanding of educational theory and practice in eighteenth-century England. Argues that Cowper's descriptions of his school years were exaggerated and unreliable and that his suggested countermeasures to the evils of public school education were impractical. Cf. Hartley, *William Cowper, Humanitarian* (348), Ch. VII, and Schmidt (816). See also 265.

Howes, Raymond F. "Cowper on Conversation" *Quarterly Journal
   of Speech*, XVIII (1932), 30-45.   [810]
   An analysis of *Conversation* in relation to the *Connoisseur*
essays, the letters, and Cowper's reading of Swift and Chesterfield.
Cf. Sherbo (817).

Hudson, Wilson M. "The Homer of the North Translates Homer,"
   Texas University Library Chronicle, IV (1950), 25-42.   [811]
   Compares translations of Homer by Alexander Pope, James
Macpherson, and Cowper.—"In competition with Pope, Cowper
succeeded far better than Macpherson."

Lindsay, Jack. "The Evangelical Magazine," *TLS*, November 12,
   1938, p. 725.   [812]
   Publication of Cowper's "Stanzas for the Northampton Bill of
Mortality for 1792" in the *Evangelical Magazine* for February,
1794."

Madan, F[alconer]. "A Newly Recovered Poem of Cowper," *TLS*,
   January 3, 1924, p. 9.   [813]
   "Who gave me grassy lawns for miry ways" reprinted from the
Common Place Book of the Hon. Lady Maitland, daughter of
Judith Madan (*nèe* Cowper).

Omond, T. S. *English Metrists* (Oxford: The Clarendon Press, 1921),
   pp. 280-281.   [814]
   A note on Cowper's "sapphics."

Roberts, W. "Cowper and the 'Times,' " *N&Q*, 9th ser., IX (January
   18, 1902), p. 47.   [815]
   "The Queen's Visit to London on the Night of the 17th of
March, 1789," in the *Times* of June 15, 1789.

Schmidt, Kuno. *Das verhalten der romantiker zur public school
   (Cowper, Shelley, Byron)* (Bonn: L. Neuendorff, 1935). (Doctoral
   dissertation.)   [816]
   Cowper's theory of public school education in *Tirocinium* in
relation to the theories of two other Romantic poets. See Hartmann (809).

Sherbo, Arthur. "Cowper's *Connoisseur* Essays," *MLN*, LXX (1955), 340-342. [817]

Relationship between Cowper's essays in the *Connoisseur* and *Conversation*. Cf. Howes (810).

Sitwell, Edith. *The English Eccentrics* (London: Faber and Faber, [1933]), pp. 302-305. [818]

Notes on the background of Cowper's "Stanzas on the late indecent Liberties taken with the remains of the great Milton."

Tennyson, Hallam. *Alfred Lord Tennyson: A Memoir* (New York: The Macmillan Company, 1897), II, 501. [819]

Tennyson's appreciation of the "exquisite flow and evenness of 'The Poplar Field' " and the "almost agonizing pathos" of the stanzas to Mary Unwin and the lines on his mother's portrait.

Van Doren, Charles Lincoln. "The Earlier Poetry of William Cowper," *Dissertation Abstracts*, XX, No. 8 (February 1960). [Abstract of a Columbia University doctoral dissertation, 1959] [820]

A critical examination of "everything that the poet wrote before 'John Gilpin' and *The Task*," considering the poetry from the point of view "of its truth to human experience" rather than in the context of the poet's time or his religious milieu. Concludes that, though some of the poetry lacks "any sort of truth," some of the verse is "much superior to most eighteenth-century verse and perhaps worthy of being considered in the canon of essential English poetry." Points out the influences of Horace and Pope and demonstrates the aptness of Saintsbury's judgment that the prosody was "in the air of another day."

Wilson, Edmund. "George Saintsbury: Gourmet and Glutton," *The New Yorker*, May 17, 1947, pp. 114-115. [821]

Comments on "Yardley Oak" and "The Castaway" as "only a little above mediocrity, as every other serious piece of Cowper's that I had ever tried to read."

Wright, Herbert G. "Cowper's 'Retirement' and Balzac's 'Entretiens,' " *MLR*, XL (1945), 129-130. [822]

Argues that the lines beginning "I praise the Frenchman" in *Retirement* (11. 739 ff.) refer not to Bruyère [La Bruyère], as Cowper suggests, but to Balzac.

G. The Letters

Bates, Madison C. "Cowper to Hayley and Rose, June 1792: Two Unpublished Letters," *Harvard Library Bulletin*, XI (1958), 80-101. [900]

Letters to William Hayley and Samuel Rose in 1792 commenting upon Mrs. Unwin's health, Hayley's generosity, and "Dr. Darwin's latest publication."

Catalogue, No. 486 (1926), Maggs Brothers, Ltd., London, lot 2086. [901]

Description of letter from Cowper "to his solicitor" written from East Barnet on March 6, 1753. Attribution questioned by Ryskamp, *William Cowper* (263), p. 183.

Cecil, Lord David. *William Cowper*, English Association Pamphlet, No. 81 (April, 1932). [902]

A lecture chiefly concerned with the letters.

Charnwood, Dorothea. "Letters by Ten Literary Men. From a Collection of Autographs," *Cornhill Magazine*, CXVIII (1918), 493. [903]

A letter to Rose dated December 1, 1791.

Chubb, E. W. "Cowper as a Letter Writer," *Stories of Authors* (New York: The Macmillan Company, 1926), pp. 42-45. [904]

A generally valueless appreciation, padded with two long quotations from the letters.—"[The letters] are interesting because [Cowper] lived a quiet life and was able in his own way to paint a picture treating of the common doings of an apparently unimportant life."

Collector [catalogue of Walter R. Benjamin, Autographs: 18 East 77th Street, New York], LXIV (April 1951), lot W 727. [905]

Extract from letter to John Duncombe, 31 December 1751, two sentences of which were transcribed in the Parke-Bernet Catalogue, No. 1190 (October 30–November 2, 1950), lot 276. Reprinted in Ryskamp (263), pp. 184-185.

"A Cowper Letter," *Antiquarian Quarterly*, I (June 1926), 178 and plate XVIII. [906]

Letter to Lady Hesketh, dated October 13, 1798.

"Cowper's Letters," *Blackwood's*, CXCII (1912), 257-262.   [907]

Review-article based on Frazer (121).—"... there was method in Cowper's very absence of method, there was art in his artlessness, or we should not be reading his letters with pleasure more than a century after they were written."

Dewar, George A. B. "Cowper the Castaway," *Saturday Review*, XCIX (1905), 12-13.   [908]

A brief review-article occasioned by the publication of Wright's *Correspondence* (151). Emphasis on the way in which the letters reflect Cowper's "life and its anguish."

De Wyzema, T. "A Propos d'un Recueil de Lettres de William Cowper," *Revue des Deux Mondes*, July 15, 1912, p. 467.   [909]

Cowper's *Letters* and Boswell's *Life of Johnson* as the two great original English works permitting readers to penetrate into human life with the most familiar intimacy.

Driver, Arthur H. "A Cowper Letter," *TLS*, July 10, 1953, p. 445.   [910]

Letter of February 25, 1791, thanking John Bacon, Esq., for a cameo.

Emden, Cecil S. *Poets in Their Letters* (New York: Oxford University Press, 1959), pp. 51-74.   [911]

A discussion of nine distinguished poets—Pope, Gray, Cowper, Wordsworth, Coleridge, Byron, Shelley, Keats, and Fitzgerald— in the light of their correspondence.—"Other poet-letter-writers of distinction have tended in this direction [self-revelation], but Cowper outstrips them all. His case is specially remarkable because he was much addicted to elaborate discussion of his personal problems, and yet was notably self-effacing in his disposition."

Glover, T. R. "Sir J. G. Frazer and the Use of Authorities," *Cambridge Review*, XXXVIII (1917), 269-270.   [912]

Frazer's edition of the letters (121) and his "coloring" of the facts.

Green, David Bonnell. "Three Cowper Letters," *N&Q*, NS III
(December, 1956), 532-534.   [913]

   A letter to John Duncombe dated November 21, 1758, and
written while Cowper was in the Temple. A letter to Joseph
Johnson dated July 19, 1786, from Olney concerning Fuseli's
criticism of Cowper's translation of Homer. A letter written from
Olney to Lady Hesketh on January 23, 1789 [90?], partially published by Hayley. (All from the Historical Society of Pennsylvania.)

Hughes, Edward. "A Letter to Thomas Wright of Durham," *Durham University Journal*, XLVI [NS XV] (1955), 65.   [914]

   Identifies the "Mr. Wright" of letter dated "Durham, November 11, 1753" (*Correspondence*, ed. Wright, I, 3-4) as Thomas
Wright, the famous Durham scientist and friend of the poet's
cousin, Spencer Cowper, Dean of Durham. But see Charles
Ryskamp, *Durham University Journal*, XLIX (1957), 126, demonstrating that the letter was written by Spencer Cowper, not
by the poet (938).

"The Hurdis-Cowper Letters. Unpublished letters addressed by
James Hurdis, the Sussex poet, to William Cowper," *Sussex
County Magazine*, April, 1927, pp. 223-225.   [915]

   See Tattersall (942).

Irvine, Lyn L. "William Cowper," *Ten Letter Writers* (London: L.
and V. Woolf, 1932), pp. 127-140.   [916]

   Sees Cowper's letters as "almost the best example in English
literature of how bricks can be made without straw." Compares
the worlds of Jane Austen and Cowper as "wedged between the
struggle of the body for life and the struggle of the mind for the
truth. The first struggle has ended and the second not begun, and
in this strange vacuum the inhabitants carry on their affairs . . .
with a precision and intentness that magnify and dignify all their
performances."

Irving, William Henry. *The Providence of Wit in the English Letter Writers* (Durham, N. C.: Duke University Press, 1955), pp. 328-359.   [917]

Walpole and Cowper as "almost the last exponents" of "atticism"—effortless limpidity and simple elegance—in English letter writing.

Joline, Adrian Hoffman. *Meditations of an Autograph Collector* (New York and London: Harper and Brothers, 1902), pp. 121-122. [918]

Reprints part of letter to "Jack" [John Duncombe] dated January 11, 1759.

————. "Meditations of an Autograph Collector," *Hobbies*, L (1945), 14.   [919]

See 918 above.

"Letters of William Cowper," *Contemporary Review*, CII (1912), 287-290.   [920]

A review-article based on Frazer (121).—"Written with all the charm and unconscious skill and playful humour of a great and lovely mind, [the letters] are an anodyne for tired souls not to be equalled in the pharmacopoeia of literature."

Lucas, E. V. "Evolution of Whimsicality," *Giving and Receiving* (New York: George H. Doran, 1922), pp. 48-63.   [921]

"Cowper [in his letters] was the first to handle the new prose . . . If Cowper was the father of whimsicality, Lamb was its chief popularizer."   See 127.

Lynd, Robert. "William Cowper," *London Mercury*, II (1920), 55-65.   [922]

Reprinted in *Living Age*, CCCVI (1920), 36-45, and in *The Art of Letters* (London: T. Fisher Unwin, 1920), pp. 65-81.—"Cowper has the charm of littleness. His life and genius were on the miniature scale, though his tragedy was a burden of Atlas."   Concerned chiefly with the perfection of the letters in contrast with the less satisfactory effect of the poetry.

Martin, Bernard. "Fresh Light on William Cowper," *MLQ*, XIII (1952), 253-255.   [923]

Repeats material published in article listed below.

————. "New Light on William Cowper," *English* (1950), 67-68.   [924]

Reports discovery of thirty-two new letters of John Newton to Cowper and purchase of six of these by the British Museum, Egerton MS 3662. (See also Martin's "Some Dissenting Friends of John Newton" in *The Congregational Quarterly* for June 1951.)

Mayor, J. E. B. "Letters of William Cowper," *N&Q*, 10th ser., II (July 2, 1904), 1-3; (July 16, 1904), 42-44; (July 30, 1904), 82-85; (August 13, 1904), 122-123; (August 27, 1904), 162-164; (September 10, 1904), 203-205; (September 24, 1904), 242-244.   [925]

Corrections and additions to Wright's edition of the *Correspondence* made from MS books of Mrs. Joseph Mayor (d. 1871) copied from MS books of Mrs. Judith Madan and her daughter, Mrs. William Cowper (*née* Maria Frances Cecelia Madan). Emendations to some of the hymns included. See 931-934.

More, Paul Elmer. "The Correspondence of William Cowper," *Shelburne Essays, Third Series* (Boston and New York: G. P. Putnam's Sons, 1905), pp. 1-27.   [926]

A review-article occasioned by Wright's edition of the *Correspondence* (151).—"The victim of his age . . . the morbid exaggeration of personal consciousness had laid hold of Cowper."

Moyer, Reed. "Letters of Gray, Walpole, and Cowper," *SR*, XIII (1905), 367-371.   [927]

"Cowper is truly Anglo-Saxon in his appreciation of homely things, in moral power, and unstudied natural style."

O'Neill, Michael J. "A Cowper Letter in Dublin," *N&Q*, NS I (January, 1954), 28.   [928]

Dated February 1, 1793, from Weston Underwood, the letter explains to unindicated addressee the state of Mrs. Unwin's health after her return from Sussex.

Parks, G. H. "A Cowper Letter," *TLS*, February 22, 1952, p. 141.   [929]

Prints a letter from Cowper to Joseph Hill, dated May 21, 1785, and "recently" found at Stoneleigh Abbey in Warwickshire. In it the poet says that he is in "a very proper mood to write

patriotic politics in a newspaper if any party or faction would be
so kind as to hire me."

Povey, Kenneth. "New Cowper Letters. I. 18th Century Dis-
cords," *Times* (London), April 25, 1930, pp. 13-14.   [930]
    See below and Pratt (935).

————. "New Cowper Letters. II. The Tragic Undercurrent,"
Times (London), April 28, 1930, pp. 15-16.   [931]
    See above.—These two articles print letters or parts of letters
omitted by Wright in the *Correspondence*. All addressed to John
Newton, they are printed from a collection of some eighty letters
presumably copied from the originals for presentation to Dr. and
and Mrs. Thomas Ring of Reading, friends of the Newtons.
Letters included are as follows: February 6, 1780 (first mention of
Madan's *Thelyphthora*); April 9, 1780 (Mr. Page's ministry at
Warrington); July 4, 1780 (relating to *Cardiphonia* and *Thelyphthora*); July 31, 1780 (the Olney bridge); May 3, 1780 (suppressed
passage on the enjoyment of nature); May 10, 1780 (suppressed
passage dealing with Cowper's conviction of damnation); September 24, 1780 ("two curious fowls"); October 29, November 11, and
December [21], 1780 (the case of the Warrington pew).

————. "Some Notes on Cowper's Letters and Poems," *RES*, V
(1929), 167-172.   [932]
    Establishes dates of six letters and shows probability of Cow-
per's authorship of six contributions to *The Annual Register*
between 1758 and 1774.

————. "The Text of Cowper's Letters," *MLR*, XXII (1927),
22-27.   [933]
    Evidence of the incompleteness and inaccuracy of all existing
collections. Prints original of letter to Hayley after his visit to
Weston in 1792 to demonstrate Hayley's alterations. See 925.

————. "Two Letters from Cowper to Greatheed," *N&Q*, CLXXVII
(July 8, 1939), 24.   [934]
    A letter dated May 26, 1793, concerns the schooling of Cow-
per's protegée, Hannah Wilson; a second endorsed by Greatheed
"Sept. 1, 1793" declines an invitation to an anniversary dinner

because of a visit from William Rose. Originals in the Liverpool Reference Library and in the private collection of Povey, respectively.

Pratt, Robert A. "Two Letters of William Cowper," *TLS*, November 19, 1931, p. 916. [935]

Letter to Newton (July 4, 1780) and another to Rose (October 4, 1789). The first was published by Povey in the London *Times* on April 25, 1930 (930) and the second was partially published by Hayley, Southey, and Wright. Both letters are in the private collection of Professor Chauncey Brewster Tinker.

Prothero, Rowland E. "Horace Walpole and William Cowper," *Quarterly Review*, CCII (1905), 35-60. [936]

A contrast occasioned by the publication of Toynbee's Letters of Horace Walpole and Wright's edition of Cowper's *Correspondence* (151).

Ryskamp, Charles. "Uncollected Letters and Essays: 1750-67," *William Cowper of the Inner Temple, Esq.* (Cambridge: Cambridge University Press, 1959), pp. 177-225. [937]

Appendix "A" to the biography. Includes letter of March 12, 1750, to Bagot ("the earliest surviving letter"); part of letter of April 1, 1752, to "Toby" [Chase Price?]; extracts from letters to John Duncombe of June 16 and December 31, 1757, and July 22, 1758; letter to *Gentleman's Magazine* of September 17, 1758; letters to John Duncombe of January 11 and June 12, 1759; letters to Joseph Hill of October 18, 1759, February 18, 1763, and April 1, 1763, *et cetera*. Demonstrates Hayley's editorial methods. Cf. 933.

————. "William Cowper and Thomas Wright," *Durham University Journal*, XLIX [NS XVIII] (1957), 126. [938]

Refutes attribution of letter to the poet. See Hughes (914).

Saintsbury, George. *A Letter Book* (London: Bell, 1922). [939]

Appreciative comment on Cowper's letters. See 388.

Saunders, E. K. "Two Unpublished Letters of Mary Unwin," *N&Q*, 12th ser., XI (December 16, 1922), 483-484. [940]

Letters to Peter Wright, a young barrister and friend of William Unwin, written before Mrs. Unwin met Cowper in 1765.

Interesting comments on the celebration of the King's Birthday and Lord Charles Montagu's ball at Huntingdon.

Strachey, Giles Lytton. "Gray and Cowper," *Characters and Commentaries* (New York: Harcourt, Brace and Company, 1933), p. 45-52. [941]

"Cowper had nothing to say, and he said it beautifully . . . His letters are stricken with sterility; they are dried up; they lack the juices of life."

Tattersall, J. F., ed. *Letters of the Reverend James Hurdis, Vicar of Bishopstone, Sussex, to William Cowper* (Bishopstone, Sussex: Privately Printed, 1927). [942]

Reprinted from the *Sussex County Magazine*, April 1927. See 915.

Thornton, Richard H. "Letter of Cowper to [Joseph] Johnson," *N&Q*, 12th ser., XI (November 18, 1922), 403. [943]

Letter written from Olney on August 6, 1781, to Cowper's publisher regarding poems later published in the 1782 volume. The letter demonstrates "Cowper's habit of beginning with a small letter after a period."

Tinker, Chauncey Brewster. *The Salon and English Letters* (New York: The Macmillan Company, 1915), pp. 197-199, 239-240, 249-250. [944]

Cowper's attempt to interest Mrs. Montagu in his *Homer*; his letters compared with those of Mme. de Sévigné and Walpole.

Tucker, William J. "Great English Letter Writers," *Catholic World*, CXLIII (1936), 695-701. [945]

Cowper in the general setting of letter writing in the eighteenth century, with emphasis on his humor: "fun as genuine and pleasurable as it is distinct from the wit of Walpole."

Vulliamy, C. E. English Letter Writers (London: Collins, 1945), pp. 25-26. [946]

"[Cowper's] letters perhaps exceed all others in beauty of style, in exquisite pathos and in luminous portrayal."

See also 205, 231, 237, 252, 337, 346, 388.

V. MISCELLANEOUS

Armstrong, T. P. "Poet's Immortality Predicted by Himself," *N&Q*, 9th ser., V (June 16, 1900), p. 481.   [1000]

Argues that the poet's prediction of his own immortality in *The Task*, II, 577 ff. was "in a very modest fashion." Compares Milton's statement on a similar subject.

"Ashley Cowper's Norfolk Poetical Miscellany (1744)," *TLS*, April 16, 1938, p. 268.   [1001]

Concerns a volume of verse by the poet's uncle.

Bayne, Thomas. "[Cowper on] Hockey [in 1785]," *N&Q*, 10th ser., I (May 4, 1904), 385.   [1002]

The game as played in the Olney streets, described in a letter to John Newton, November 5, 1785.

———. "Cowper: Pronunciation of His Name," *N&Q*, 10th ser., XII (October 2, 1909), 265-266.   [1003]

Comment on Lowell's rhyming Cowper's name with "horse-trooper" in *A Fable for Critics*, with replies by J. N. Dowling, *ibid.* (October 23, 1909), 335-336; W. W. Skeat (November 6, 1909), 372; F. Newman and G. W. E. R. (November 27, 1909), 432-433; U. J. D. (December 25, 1909), 516-517; also 12th ser. VIII (March 19, 1921), 237; (April 9, 1921), 299; (April 23, 1921), 338; (May 7, 1921), 377. See also 1025.

Boston, Noel. "Cowper Celebrations," *TLS*, April 25, 1952, p. 281.   [1004]

Celebrations in honor of the poet in East Dereham.

Clark, Harry Hayden, ed. *Transitions in American Literary History* (Durham, N. C.: Duke University Press, 1953), p. 130. [1005]
Imitators of Cowper in America.

Dodgson, Edward S. "Did Cowper Write 'The School of Virtue' (London: 1897)?" *Antiquary*, LI (1915), 53-57. [1006]
A preposterous attempt to prove Cowper's authorship of an obscure novel by resorting to stylistic comparison and other forms of assumed internal evidence.

"Fama," *pseud.* "Judith Cowper, Mrs. Madan," *N&Q*, 12th ser., X (February 4, 1922), 95. [1007]
Ascribes the "Abelard to Eloisa" usually attributed to William Pattison (see *N&Q*, 11th ser., X, 27, 97) to Judith Madan, aunt of William Cowper and friend of Pope.

Flowers, Desmond, and A. N. L. Munby, eds. *English Poetical Autographs* (London: Transatlantic Arts, 1938). [1008]
Includes an autograph of a poem of Cowper.

Gray, W. Forbes. "Cowper and Flying Machines," *Fortnightly*, CLXI (1947), 68-69. [1009]
See Parsons (1016) and *Spectator*, CIII (July 31, 1909), 162 (1017).

Jarrell, Randall. *Pictures from an Institution* (New York: Alfred A. Knopf, 1954), pp. 108-110. [1010]
A contemporary poet, critic, and novelist comments obliquely on Cowper's literary reputation.

Mabbott, Thomas Olive. "The Miltonic Epitaph on Mazarin: Cowper's Opinion," *N&Q*, CLXXII (1937), 188. [1011]
Confirms judgment of "most modern students of Milton" that the epitaph is rightly ascribed to him.

Mott, Frank Luther. *Golden Multitudes, The Story of Best Sellers in the United States* (New York: The Macmillan Company, 1947), pp. 46-48. [1012]
The popularity of Cowper in America.—"In general, the literary critics were lukewarm toward Cowper, or worse; but the common people loved him." See 1014.

————. *A History of American Magazines* (Cambridge, Massachusetts: Harvard University Press, 1939), I, 178, 293.   [1013]

Notes on evidences of Cowper's vogue in America.

Newton, Annabel. *Wordsworth in Early American Criticism* (Chicago: University of Chicago Press, 1928), pp. 103, 175 ff.   [1014]

Evidences of high regard for Cowper in early American criticism. Cf. Mott (1012).

O'Donoghue, F. M. "On a Portrait of William Cowper," *Home Counties Magazine*, II (1900), 1.   [1015]

For other articles on Cowper iconography, see Povey (1018), Roberts (1020) and Ryskamp (1023).

Parsons, Howard. "Milton and the Aeroplane," *N&Q*, CXCIV (1951), 372.   [1016]

Notes Cowper's prophecy of flight in "Boadicea." See Gray (1009) and below (1017).

"Poet's Views on Aviation," *Spectator*, CIII (July 31, 1909), 162. [1017]

See Gray (1009) and above (1016).

[Povey, Kenneth]. "Lawrence and Cowper," *Times* (London), May 6, 1930, p. 19.   [1018]

Concerns the "lost" Lawrence portrait of the poet. See O'Donoghue (1015) and Ryskamp (1023).

Quinlan, Maurice J. *Victorian Prelude: A History of English Manners, 1700-1830* (New York: Columbia University Press, 1941), pp. 52-53.   [1019]

Cowper's part in furthering the Evangelical cause.

Roberts, W. "Romney's Portrait of Cowper," *Athenaeum*, No. 3773 (February 17, 1900), pp. 215-216.   [1020]

Argues that the Romney painting sold in 1894 at Christie's as "A Head (possibly Cowper)" and later presented to the National Portrait Gallery by Sir Robert Scharf is not, in fact, a portrait of Cowper. See Bailey, *Poems* (104), xv-xvii.

Rusk, Ralph L. *Literature of the Middle Western Frontier* (New York: Columbia University Press, 1925), II, 11 *n*. [1021]

Cites instances of the early appearance of Cowper's works in backwoods America.

Ryskamp, Charles. "Blake's Cowperian Sketches," *RES*, IX (1958), 48-49. [1022]

A note on Blake's pen-and-ink and aquamarine wash drawings of Hayley's design for the proposed monument to Cowper at East Dereham. See Keynes (433).

———. "Lawrence's Portrait of Cowper," *The Princeton University Library Chronicle*, XX (1959), 140-145, and two plates. [1023]

Identifies a pencil and wash sketch of Cowper found in the Cowper Museum as the "lost" portrait by Lawrence. See Povey (1018).

Sibley, Agnes M. *Alexander Pope's Prestige in America, 1725-1835* (New York: King's Crown Press, 1949), p. 100. [1024]

Comments on comparative reputation of Pope, Cowper, and Wordsworth, suggesting that "romantics looked in vain in the pages of Pope for something to satisfy the thirst of their souls" and that "Cowper . . . far more than Wordsworth, was the ideal poet of nineteenth-century America."

Sturge, Joseph. "The Cowper Centenary," *Listener*, VI (July 1, 1931), 31. [1025]

A brief note on the pronunciation of Cowper's name by a correspondent who, as a child, had met an old man who had actually known the poet in Olney. See 1003.

Van Dyke, Tertius [Noble]. "Crazy Kate," New York *Times*, March 6, 1936, p. 10. [Editorial page.] [1026]

An original poem based on the well-known passage in *The Task*, I, 534 ff.

Walpole, Horace. *Correspondence with the Reverend William Cole*, edited by Wilmarth S. Lewis and A. D. Wallace (New Haven: Yale University Press, 1937), II, 302, 307-309. [1027]

Walpole's effort to get an etching of John Cowper, the poet's brother, made by the Reverend Michael Tyson.

Warner, S. Allen. "A Cowper Relic," *TLS*, September 23, 1955, p. 557. [1028]

Twigs from Cowper's garden and the putative "scarlet mantle warm" of Cowper's mother, formerly in possession of Yardley Warner (1815-1855), an American Quaker who devoted most of his life to Negro emancipation and to education.

INDEX OF NAMES

(References are to page numbers)

Trent, William P., 100
Tucker, W. J., 147
Tupper, James Waddell, 85
Turner, W. J., 122
Tyson, Reverend Michael, 151

Unwin, Mary, 5, 28, 57, 58, 61, 66, 70, 91, 96, 101, 122, 139, 140, 144, 146
Unwin, William, 27, 55, 56, 72, 92, 146

Van Doren, Charles L., 139
Van Doren, Mark, 47, 49, 85
Van Dyke, T. N., 151
Vaughan, Henry, 37, 125
Vincent, J., 132
Vine, Sherrard, 122
Voltaire, 123
Vulliamy, C. E., 147

Wake, Joan, 132
Wallace, A. D., 151
Waller, 57
Walpole, Horace, 46, 50, 143, 144, 146, 147, 151
Walpole, Sir Hugh, 109
Ward, A. C., 132
Warner, Charles Dudley, 85
Warner, S. A., 152
Warner, Yardley, 152
Warren, C. H., 122
Watts, Isaac, 126
Waugh, Arthur, 122
Webb, W. T., 85

Weiss, Harry B., 132
Wells, John Edwin, 132
Wesley, John, 72, 75
Westacott, Charles Albert, 100
Whibley, Charles, 62
Whitefield, George, 72
Whitehead, Charles, 20
Whiting, Mary Bradford, 100
Whitney, Lois, 80
Whittier, John Greenleaf, 8-9
Williams, William Carlos, 71
Willis, William, 101
Wilson, Edmund, 13, 139
Wilson, Hannah, 145
Wood, Frederick T., 122
Wood, Paul Spencer, 84
Woodbury, George E., 123
Woods, George Benjamin, 86
Woolf, Virginia, 12, 101
Wordsworth, William, 4, 10, 11, 13, 64, 68, 70, 119, 125, 135, 151
Wormhoudt, Arthur, 136
Wright, G. W., 101
Wright, H. G., 126, 139
Wright, John, 101
Wright, Thomas, 17, 20, 22-23, 46, 48, 49, 75, 85, 86, 101, 144
Wright, Thomas (of Durham), 142, 146

Yardley, E., 126
Young, Edward, 9, 37, 125
Young, Sir George, 123
Young, Kenneth, 96